Tax Guide 201

INVESTOR GAINS & LOSSES

by

Holmes F. Crouch
Tax Specialist

Published by

Allyear Tax Guides
**20484 Glen Brae Drive
Saratoga, CA 95070**

ISBN   0-944817-09-2

LCN 92-73883

Printed in U.S.A.

Series 200
Investors and Businesses

Tax Guide 201

INVESTOR GAINS & LOSSES

For other titles in print, see page 224.

The author: **Holmes F. Crouch**
For more about the author, see page 221.

PREFACE

If you are a **taxpayer** whose income exceeds $40,000 per year, this book can be helpful to you. It is designed to be read — from cover to cover — in less than six hours. Or, you can skim read it in approximately 30 minutes.

Either way, you are treated to **tax knowledge** . . . *beyond the ordinary*. The "beyond" is that which you cannot find in official instructions, and that which is not ordinarily imparted to you by professional counselors.

Taxpayers have different levels of interest in a selected tax subject. For this reason, this book starts with introductory fundamentals and progresses through some rather complex situations. You can verify the progression by chapter and section in the table of contents. In the text, "applicable law" is quoted in pertinent part. Key interpretive phrases and key tax forms are emphasized. Real-life examples are given . . . in down-to-earth style.

This book has 12 chapters. This number provides depth without cross-subject rambling. Each chapter starts with a head summary of meaningful information.

To overcome the humdrum of ordinary tax jargon, informative diagrams and tables are placed strategically throughout the text. Most of the illustrations are true originals. By leafing through page by page, reading the summaries and section headings, and glancing at the diagrams and tables, you can get a good handle on the matters covered.

Effort has been made to update and incorporate all of the latest tax law changes that are significant to the title subject. However, "beyond the ordinary" does not encompass every conceivable variant of fact and law that might give rise to protracted dispute and litigation. Consequently, if a particular statement or paragraph is crucial to your own specific case, you are urged to seek professional counseling. Otherwise, the information presented is general and is designed for a broad range of reader interests.

The Author

INTRODUCTION

This book is for the serious investor who is annoyed — perhaps irritated — by the avalanche of "information returns" (Forms 1099 and K-1) that he receives each year concerning his investments. The fact is, today, *each and every* investment transaction made by an individual is electronically reported to the IRS for maximum taxing purposes. This is the consequence of **Section 6045** of the Internal Revenue Code on broker and payer reportings.

There is a very interesting and unpublicized phenomenon concerning the Section 6045 reportings. Only positive income is reported: interest, dividends, capital gains, and gross proceeds. Losses are not reported, and, if they were to be, the IRS ignores all losses. You could make a $10,000 investment, and roll it over three times with no gain or loss. At the end of the year, your broker would report $30,000 to the IRS. Unless you are tax vigilant — we'll tell you how to be so herein — the IRS will computer tax you on the entire $30,000!

We all know that investing is a two-sided coin. On one side, there may be gains. They may be either capital gains or ordinary gains. Each type is tax treated differently. We'll explain later. *Hint*: capital gains are treated more favorably than ordinary gains.

The other side of the investment coin is the loss side. Losses, too, are tax characterized as either capital losses or ordinary losses. Ordinary losses are treated more favorably than capital losses.

Our investment coin also has a border (or edge). In tax jargon, this is called: *cost or other basis*. If you religiously keep track of your costs (which are distinguished from "expenses"), and make the proper allocations and adjustments as you go along, your cost (as adjusted) becomes **return of capital**. This is NOT TAXED.

But how good are your investment records and how good is your understanding of the gain/loss rules, when the IRS starts inundating you with its computer-matching demands? Poor records and poor understandings mean high tax. It's just that simple.

Anticipating and waiting for lower tax rates on capital gains (as was the case prior to 1987), will not help your computer-matching burdens one iota. The IRS's computer does not know — and does not care — when you acquired each capital asset. It (the computer) only cares when you sell . . . or exchange . . . or otherwise dispose of each investment. Lower-than-regular rates on capital gains mean

greater — NOT less — recordkeeping with respect to short-, intermediate-, and long-term holdings.

Instead of being an investor, have you put money, property, or services into a sports, hobby, or recreational-type activity? If so, the *not-for-profit* presumption applies. This means that your cost adjustments and expense deductions are disallowed, and your loss is tax ignored.

As an investor (explained in Chapter 1), if you get nothing else out of this book, we think you'll at least begin to feel comfortable and familiar with the four most important tax forms that attach to your annual Form 1040. For investors, these important forms are:

Schedule B — Interest and Dividend Income
Schedule D — Capital Gains and Losses
Schedule E — Supplemental Income and Loss
Form 4797 — Sales of Business Property

To be sure, there are other auxiliary forms that you may need, but you could get by with those above.

To aid in our analysis of the tax rules for you, we have classified all investments into such groupings as: (1) Sterile assets, (2) Portfolio assets, (3) Conduit assets, (4) Rental real estate, (5) Section 1231 property, and (6) Special situations. Within each grouping, of course, there are separate assets. This means that each asset — item by item, account by account, or property by property — needs to be "cost trailed" separately: **not** as a group.

Upon the disposition of each asset (by sale, exchange, or otherwise), precise gain/loss tax computations — and reportings — are required. This is so, whether you invest locally, nationally, or globally. For long-held assets, inflation indexing can be an adjustment to your cost.

Gone are the days when you could invest your money any way you wanted, without Big Brother — the IRS — looking over your shoulder. We are truly sorry about this. It is the price we all pay for the utopia of total computer control of our financial lives. But with due diligence and care, you can turn the system around and use it constructively for your own tax benefit. We'll tell you how, in the chapters which follow.

CONTENTS

1

INVESTOR DEFINED

An Investor Is One Who Advances Money To Acquire A Capital Asset In Which He Exercises Primarily A Passive Role. Upon Disposition Of The Asset, There May Be Capital Gain Or Capital Loss. Either Way He Pays No Social Security Tax On The Gross Proceeds. While Holding An Asset, It May Or May Not Generate Income Or Loss; If It Does, "Current" Accounting Is Required And Special Rules Apply. Otherwise, An Investor Must "Capitalize" His Costs To Establish His Tax Basis At Time Of Sale. A Solvent Investor Always Has Flexibility Of Choice When Disposing Of His Asset(s) For Recovery Of His Money.

Most persons who have ever invested money, or intend to, have heard of the "stock market." This is that process whereby one invests money through a stock broker to buy X number of shares in the ABC corporation. The investor then sits back and bides his time. By doing so, he hopes to make a million dollars ($1,000,000) on his investment.

If his X number of shares increases in value by $1,000,000 — which would be rare indeed — and he sells those shares, he then has capital gain income. He has to report and pay tax on this income by a separate accounting process.

Suppose, now, instead of making a million dollars, our investor lost $1,000,000 in the ABC corporation. Instead of a capital gain, he has a capital loss. How is he taxed on this loss?

As we will see later, he is taxed much differently — and much less favorably — on losses than on gains.

Within this scenario, we have all of the qualifying elements of what constitutes an investor for capital gain/capital loss tax purposes. Included also is the realization that certain gain/loss computations will produce ordinary gain (due to recapture rules) or ordinary loss (due to recharacterization rules).

In this introductory chapter, therefore, we want to dwell strictly on the characteristics of what constitutes an investor. If one qualifies properly, certain tax accounting benefits accrue. If one does not qualify, he is taxed higher on his gains than he need be, and his losses may not be tax recognized.

Passivity: The Main Key

There is one key, basic characteristic that distinguishes an investor from all other taxpayers. He plays a purely passive role in the management of capital assets. Any active role therewith is performed solely by market forces . . . over the passage of time.

An investor makes the decision to acquire a capital asset. Once he does so, he sits back and observes the market fluctuations in the value of that asset. Time passes. As it does, an investor may take, or be given, "snapshots" of the condition of his asset. Other than occasional observations, he does not significantly participate in its day-to-day happenings. Someone else, or some entity, does. Then, at some later point in time, an investor decides to sell or otherwise dispose of his asset.

The passivity role of an investor does not mean that he puts up his money then forgets about it. It simply means that he does not participate actively in the market place in a direct manner. That is, he exercises no direct influence on the change in value of his asset with time. He may repair and maintain his asset, or even improve it, but otherwise he is purely on the sidelines. He hardly turns a hand to influence its gain or loss.

In essence, then, an investor puts money into an asset, watches it gain or lose, and decides when to sell/dispose of that asset. His active attention consists of three distinct phases, namely:

Phase I   — The mental decision to buy
Phase II   — The emotional observation over time
Phase III — The mental decision to sell

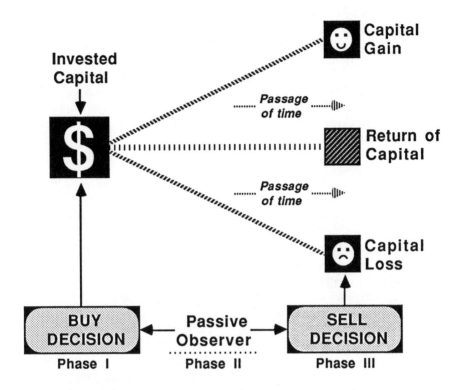

Fig. 1.1 - Passivity: The Primary Characteristic of an Investor

We present these characteristic phases in Figure 1.1.

Using Figure 1.1 as a background reference, let us give a simple example of the passivity role of an investor. Take a gold bullion coin.

A gold coin is a pure — and sterile — investment asset. It does not earn income; it does not change in size and shape. It does not tarnish and it does not wear out on its own. It cannot be eaten or otherwise consumed in productive enterprise. Once formed it stays fixed (even over thousands of years) until purposely destroyed by melting it down.

An investor buys a gold coin and puts it in his dresser drawer. Certainly, he did some research on where to buy and on what type of coin to buy. But this is a decision-making process of his own. In the dresser drawer, the coin is dormant. The investor himself can do nothing to influence the value of the coin with the passage of time. Market forces entirely beyond his control influence the coin's value while it is being held as an investment.

Sometime later, the investor takes his coin out of the drawer, and sells it. Again, a mental decision is required to do this. And, of course, he would do some shopping around among coin dealers and brokers to get the best price that he could. Whether he gets more money back, or less money back than he paid, will depend on market factors over time. As to these market factors, the role of the coin investor was truly passive.

No Social Security Tax

Why is passivity so important to an investor?

Because if he makes a gain, gets his money back, or suffers a loss, there is no Social Security/Medicare tax to pay!

The Social Security/Medicare tax is one of the most insidious taxes of modern time. It starts with the very first dollar of *personal participation* income. It is a fixed percentage each year, which increases year after year. It applies to a specified "participation base" which also increases year after year. Against the first and subsequent participation base dollars, there are no offsets for adjustments, deductions, and expenses. Politically, it is called a "contribution," but administratively it is called a "tax" (to make it compulsory). One is compelled to pay Social Security/Medicare tax on (virtually) every personal participation dollar that he makes.

Because of his passive role in the making or losing of dollars, an investor pays no Social Security/Medicare tax on his investment proceeds. For those assets towards which he takes on an active personal service role, he *does* pay the tax. The Social Security/Medicare tax is a *second* tax on personal service income. Hence, passivity in connection with one's investment assets is the distinguishing feature that relieves one from such tax.

The Social Security system is not a voluntary matter at all. If one is employed or self-employed, he is mandated to pay into the system. This is supposed to be a "contribution." Because it is a contributions tax, it is referred to in the Internal Revenue Code as "other taxes."

For employees, Section 3101(a) of the Internal Revenue Code applies. This section carries the official heading: **Old-age, survivors, and disability insurance.** The introductory wording therein reads—

In addition to other taxes, there is hereby imposed on the income of every individual a tax equal to the [designated] *percentage of the wages . . . received by him with respect to employment.* [Emphasis added.]

For self-employeds, Section 1401(a) applies. This section carries the same official heading as Section 3101(a) above. The introductory wording of Section 1401(a) reads—

In addition to other taxes, there shall be imposed for each taxable year, on the self-employment income of every individual, a tax equal to the [designated] *percent of the amount of the self-employment income for such taxable year.*

If an investor becomes too active in his wheelings and dealings, day to day, he crosses the threshold into the domain of a self-employed participant (in the market place). When he does so, the Social Security/Medicare tax promptly applies. A true investor is neither employed in the business of making investments nor self-employed therein. His capital alone does the work.

"Trade or Business" Explained

To avoid paying Social Security/Medicare tax on investment proceeds, an investor must not be in a trade or business (with his invested money). What constitutes a trade or business, therefore, should be explained.

Basically, a trade or business is a pursuit carried on for livelihood via profit. That is, one engages in an activity on a regular basis to produce income and livelihood. To produce a livelihood, one needs to make a *profit, more or less regularly.* If no net profit is made in a reasonable span of time, one quits that pursuit and, perhaps, starts another. One's livelihood derives from the profits made: not from the losses incurred.

The pursuit of a livelihood means that one is engaged in a trade or business, whose products or services are offered to the public at large. The offerings are made every business day — or virtually every business day — on a continuing basis. The offerings are made to customers and clients who pay a price, commission, or fee for the products or services accepted. These "gross receipts," as they are called, derive strictly from the acumen and skill of the entrepreneur: *not* from the mere passage of time. Certainly, in a trade or business, one must invest money in certain assets (buildings, equipment, inventory, labor, merchandise, etc.) in order to make a profit and derive income.

It is true that an investor also invests money with the intention of making a profit. Seldom does an investor intentionally want to lose money. But it is doubtful that the profit motive in passive investments is essential to one's livelihood. In fact, an adage of investment wisdom states: "Do not invest money that you cannot afford to lose. And do not invest money for your sole source of livelihood."

The investment world and a trade or business are two different ballgames. Investors speak of "gross proceeds" whereas proprietors refer to gross receipts. From their gross proceeds, investors determine their "gain or loss" of capital. In contrast, proprietors determine their "profit or loss" of income. An investor does not depend on the "bottom line" for his livelihood, whereas a proprietor does.

Borderline Examples

The distinction between an investor and being in a trade or business is important not only for Social Security/Medicare tax purposes, but also for cost and expense accounting reasons. Let us illustrate the distinction with three examples: a stock broker, a land owner, and an antique clock collector.

A stock broker is a person in the trade or business of buying and selling stocks, bonds, and securities for other persons than himself. He does this on a day-to-day basis for his clients. But he also may buy/sell some of the same stock and securities for his own account. How does he distinguish his own investments from the trading of investments for his clients?

Answer: A special tax law applies. It is Section 1236(a) of the tax code. Its heading is: **Dealers in securities: Capital gains.** The wording therein reads as follows—

> *Gain by a dealer in securities from the sale or exchange of any security shall in no event be considered as gain from the sale or exchange of a capital asset unless—*
> *(1) the security was, before the close of the day on which it was acquired . . . , clearly identified in the dealer's records as a security held for investment; and*

(2) the security was not, at any time after the close of the day (or such earlier time), held by such dealer primarily for sale to customers in the ordinary course of his trade or business.

So, a stock broker has to clearly identify his own investments and keep a separate, detailed record of them. Both of the Section 1236(a) requirements must be met. Otherwise any gain on his own transactions is treated as ordinary income subject to the Social Security/Medicare tax.

In the case of a land owner, the distinction between holding land for investment purposes and for sale to customers in a trade or business is more difficult. Consider, for example, that a person bought a 50-acre tract of land. He decides to subdivide the tract into 1-acre parcels and sell them off a few at at time. Is he an investor, or is he a developer?

Another section of the tax code addresses this situation. This is Section 1237(a), headed as: **Real property subdivided for sale.** Pertinent excerpts read—

*Any lot or parcel which is a part of a tract of real property in the hands of a taxpayer **other than a corporation** shall not be deemed to be held primarily for sale to customers in the ordinary course of trade or business at the time of sale solely because of the taxpayer having subdivided such tract for purposes of sale or because of any activity incident to such subdivision or sale if—*

*(1) such tract, or any lot or parcel thereof, had not been previously held by such taxpayer primarily for sale to customers . . .; **and***

*(2) no substantial improvement that substantially enhances the value of the lot or parcel sold is made by the taxpayer . . .; **and***

(3) such lot or parcel, except in the case of real property acquired by inheritance or devise, is held by the taxpayer for a period of 5 years. [Emphasis added.]

Section 1237 is quite lengthy. It details special rules for its application. It defines the minimum number of parcel sales for capital gain purposes. It defines "necessary improvements" and "expenditures of sale." The subdivision of land for sale is a vast area of Tax Court litigation over capital gain versus ordinary gain. With the Social Security/Medicare tax rates so high these days, and with the taxable base (virtually) unlimited in amount, paying the "second tax" on real property investment gains is a horrifying example of taxes-on-taxes running wild.

In the case of an antique clock collector, other special tax rules apply. Is the person an investor; is he a hobbyist; or is he a dealer? It all depends. He is taxed differently in each case.

Suppose the collector bought one or two antique clocks which were in need of repair. He had them professionally refurbished. Shortly thereafter, he offered them for sale at a profit. If this is all he did, he would be an investor. No Social Security/Medicare tax would apply.

Suppose he bought numerous old clocks, and did the repairs and renovations himself. He hung the clocks up in various rooms of his home. He showed them off frequently to his friends and guests. Occasionally, he would sell one or two to his friends, to get cash to buy other old clocks. He is a hobbyist. Section 183 would apply, namely: **Activities not engaged in for profit**. His expenses would be allowable only to the extent of his sales receipts, each year. If a net gain, he would pay Social Security/Mecicare tax. If a net loss, the loss would not be tax recognized.

If the collector bought and sold refurbished antique clocks frequently, advertised them regularly, and serviced the ones that he sold, he would be a dealer. Such activities are clearly a trade or business serving the general public. He would show an "operating" profit or loss at the end of each year. The profit is Social Security/Mecicare taxed; the loss is tax recognized. The loss can be used to offset other taxable sources of income.

Phase II "Income" Classes

If you glance back at Figure 1.1 for a moment, you'll see that Phase II sort of "hangs in there." Our attention at the time was focused on Phase I (acquisition of an investment asset) and Phase III (disposition of it). Between Phase I and Phase III, there was passage of time which we called Phase II. This is the observation-over-time phase which, in the tax world of investments, is called *holding period*. We'll see in later chapters that the length of the holding period has a material bearing on the tax treatment of capital gains and capital losses.

During the holding-period phase, some investments generate income. Sterile investments do not generate income, but most other investments do . . . in one form or another. Sterile investments are gold coins, precious metals, commodities, collectibles (stamps, guns, antiques, works of art, etc.), raw land, and personal-use assets. These are "sterile" in the sense that they generate no tax-accountable income while being held.

Tax accountable income — and in some cases loss — during the holding period is NOT the type of gains and losses that we are dwelling on in this book. But we have to tell you about this income or loss so that you can properly classify and costify your investments at the time of their disposition. The reason that we have to do this is that the tax treatment at disposition differs, depending on the income generated during holding. All income — and certain losses — during holding are tax accounted for separately and distinctly from gain or loss at time of disposition. There are two different tax accounting ballgames going on here.

With certain tax-accounting differences in mind, the classes of holding-period income are:

Class I — Portfolio income
• interest and dividends from depository accounts, loans, bonds, stocks, and other securities (paper assets)

Class II — Passive activity income
• that from limited partnerships, S corporations, estates, trusts, and investment pools (conduit assets)

Class III — Participative income
• that from rental and royalty property where the investor is the owner or co-owner thereof (tangible assets)

We depict these three investment-income classes in Figure 1.2. For completeness, we also include a "Class O," to represent the sterile assets. We'll amplify on each of the three income classes in the paragraphs below. None of the income is subject to the Social Security/Medicare tax.

Portfolio Income

In simplistic terms, portfolio income consists of interest and dividends derived from purely paper assets. That is, the investor does not own directly or indirectly any of the underlying assets which generate said interest or dividends. He holds a *paper contract* which, if push comes to shove, is enforceable under law. It is this

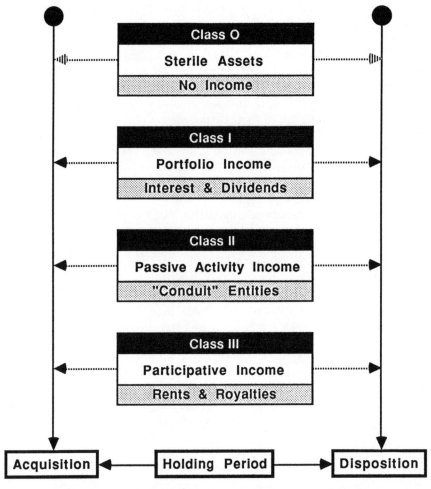

Fig. 1.2 - Income Classes of Investment Assets

holding of paper contracts that gives rise to the term "portfolio" income.

Interest is the price paid per unit of time for the use of money. This includes the price paid for the creditors' (investors') forbearance in demanding payment on money loaned, and for any payment made to postpone the payment of interest. It also includes original issue discounts, if any. In short, interest is the income generated from the renting of money to others. Interest is usually paid monthly.

Dividends are distributions of property made by a corporation to its shareholders. The distributions are made from the accumulated or current earnings and profits of the corporation. To constitute dividends, however, the distributions must be made during the ordinary course of the corporate business. The distributions (dividends) may be in the form of money, securities, or property. If other than money, the fair market value of the securities or property distributed must be established. Dividends are usually paid quarterly.

Interest is usually at a fixed rate during the period of holding. At the end of the holding period, the investor expects to get his initial principal (capital) back. This may not always happen, but this is the expectation.

In contrast, the rate of dividend payments varies from time to time, during the period of holding. The holder of a dividend-bearing asset, since he is sharing in the earnings and profits of the corporation, hopes, but does not necessarily expect, to get all of his money back at the end of the holding period. He may get more back; he may get less back; or he may get none back.

Interest and dividends, when paid, are all positive sources of income to the investor. There are no negative (loss) payments of interest, nor negative (loss) payments of dividends. The amount of payments may be reduced, but they are never negative in the accounting sense. This is an important distinction for the tax treatment of portfolio income.

Passive Activity Income

Passive activity income (or loss) is that which is derived from money, securities, or property contributed to conduit entities. There are four general classes of these entities, namely:

1. Limited Partnerships
   — legal liability is limited to the monetary amount invested
2. S Corporations
   — investor is one of 35 or less shareholders
3. Estates and Trusts
   — where the executor/trustee makes the investments on behalf of beneficiaries
4. Real Estate Mortgage Pools

— investor is one of 100 or more "associates" who pool money for real estate and mortgage-backed securities

These four classes of entities are referred to as "conduits" because they are tax allowed to pass through to each investor his pro rata share of income, losses, gains, credits, and deductions. Each investor, thereby, is on his own to use the pass-through amounts in whatever way is most tax beneficial to him. This pass-through feature makes conduit entities particularly attractive as tax shelters.

Conduit entities can engage in all kinds of trade or business activities, as well as dealing in securities, mineral property, oil and gas exploration, farming syndication, equipment leases, real estate, and other (speculative) activities. Losses as well as gains from these activities are passed through to the investors.

All investments in conduit entities, however, are subject to two special tax rules. These rules are:

Sec. 465 — Deduction limited to amount at risk
Sec. 469 — Passive activities losses and credits limited

Section 465 says, in essence, that if an investor puts up $10,000 out of his own pocket (or from loans for which he is personally liable), he can never write off more than $10,000. Should his distributive share of cumulative deduction exceed his $10,000, the excess is "suspended" until the entity generates positive income. At that point, his suspended deductions may be used to offset his distributive-share income. This at-risk limitation holds throughout the holding period, and includes termination of the entity.

Section 469 says, in essence, that for any given year, the passthrough losses and credits cannot exceed the positive income and gain for that year. The unused losses and credits are carried over to subsequent taxable years, where they can be used to offset any positive income and gains in those years. This can go on until the entity is liquidated, at which time the cumulative unused losses cannot exceed the cumulative amounts at risk.

Participative Income

Participative income is that which is derived from the ownership or co-ownership of property by the individual investor(s). No intermediate entity is involved. For practical reasons, the number of co-owners is generally limited to five investors (a husband and wife count as one investor). In most cases, a husband and wife own the investment property outright, or they and one other couple own it. The property produces rent and royalties which are shared among the co-owners.

The property rented to others may be machinery and equipment, residential real estate, commercial real estate, farm land, mineral-resource land, oil and gas rights, hunting and fishing resorts, and so on. Income is produced and expenses are incurred. The expense deductions also include depreciation, depletion, and amortization.

Rental and royalty income to the investor(s)/owner(s) is called "participative" income. This is because the owner(s)/investor(s) have to participate in making management decisions, such as approving tenants, deciding on rental terms, making improvements, overseeing maintenance and repairs, and negotiating equipment leases and royalty contracts.

Taxwise, the property management decisions are treated as *active participation*. This, in concept, is far short of "material participation" which crosses the border into an active trade or business (where the Social Security/Medicare tax applies). The reason that active participation is not subject to this tax is that the income derives predominantly from the use of the property itself, rather than deriving from the personal service(s) of the owner(s)/investor(s) themselves. Rental/royalty property is usually based on contractual-use periods of one year or more. Consequently, day-to-day participative attention is not required.

The active-participation aspect of rental/royalty property qualifies for a limited exemption to the passive-activity-loss rule of Section 469. Instead of any losses being limited to the income generated each year, *rental real estate* is allowed a $25,000 net loss exemption. [Sec. 469(i)(1), (2), (3).] This net loss exemption "phases out" when one's total gross income from all sources exceeds $100,000 (for each taxable year). Thus, for small investors, rental real estate has some attractive holding-period tax advantages.

De Minimis Personal Use

Another characteristic of an investor is no or negligible personal use of the asset in which his money is invested. The word "negligible" does not appear in the tax code. In its place, the phrase *de minimis* is used.

For tax purposes, de minimis means an amount which is—

> *. . . so small as to make accounting for it unreasonable or administratively impracticable.* [Sec. 132(e)(1).]

In quantitative terms, de minimis means less than 5% in value, time, or services. Any personal use of an asset 5% or more triggers precise allocation accounting rules, which can virtually wipe out its investment advantages.

The point is that in order to maintain the investment character of an asset, one should not use his investments for personal pleasure or for other personal-use purposes. Any personal use severely limits the allowable costs in that asset, and denies all capital-loss treatment, should the asset be sold at a loss.

Personal-use assets encompass such items as one's home, car, furniture, pleasure vehicles (boat, airplane, camper), equipment (personal computers), furnishings (paintings, silverware), jewelry, stamp collections, gun collections, and the like. True, these are investments in a sense, but investing for profit is not the primary purpose for their acquisition. One generally acquires a personal capital asset for his personal living, enjoyment, and recreation.

Furthermore, there is no passivity towards such assets. Every day (almost), the owner/holder of personal-use assets changes, improves, rearranges, uses, damages, repairs, and otherwise personally "wears and tears" them. There is very little observational passivity, as in the case of a true investor.

If a personal capital asset is sold at a loss, one gets neither capital loss treatment nor ordinary loss treatment. The loss is simply not tax recognized. It is a pure personal loss with no tax benefit whatsoever. There are no gains/loss offsets of any kind.

Not Related Taxpayers

No person nor entity likes to lose when disposing of a capital asset. Consequently, when a loss is anticipated, there is a natural desire to want to transfer the asset within one's circle of relationships so that the reduced value of the asset benefits some one or some entity of choice, rather than benefiting a remote third party. In some cases, losses are actually contrived so that the transferor may claim a capital loss.

There is a no-no rule which says that losses on capital transactions between related taxpayers are not recognized. It makes no difference whether the assets are held for personal use, business use, or for investment purposes. If the taxpayers are related in any way, the capital losses are not recognized.

The tax law on point is Section 267: **Losses with respect to transactions between related taxpayers.** Section 267(a) reads in part as follows—

No deduction shall be allowed in respect of any loss from the sale or exchange of property, directly or indirectly, between persons specified in any of the paragraphs of subsection (b).

Subsection (b) consists of 12 paragraphs. The gist of these paragraphs is to define related taxpayers as:

1. Members of a family.
2. An individual and a corporation in which he owns more than 50% of the stock in each.
3. Two corporations which are members of the same controlled group.
4. A grantor and a fiduciary of a trust.
5. Two fiduciaries of trusts, with a common grantor.
6. A fiduciary and a beneficiary of a trust.
7. A fiduciary of one trust and a beneficiary of another trust, with a common grantor.
8. A fiduciary and a trust and a corporation where the grantor of the trust owns more than 50% of the corporate stock.
9. A person and an exempt organization controlled by members of the same family.
10. A corporation and a partnership if the same persons own more than 50% of each entity.
11. An "S" corporation and another "S" corporation of the same persons.
12. An "S" corporation and a "C" corporation of the same persons.

As you skimmed these 12 paragraphs of related taxpayers, you may have noted a thread of commonality. In all cases, there is a common economic control or substantial influence. There are no adversarial interests. The commonality of influence may be between two persons, between a person and an entity, or between two entities. Whatever the arrangement, or for whatever the reason, if capital transaction losses are sustained, they are not tax recognized.

If the capital asset is subsequently sold by the related taxpayer at a gain, the gain is first reduced by the nonrecognized loss. Thereupon, the capital gain rules apply. In a sense, therefore, the initial losses are semirecognized on the second sale or exchange.

What the above means, in essence, is that any capital transaction between related taxpayers is suspect. The suspicion prevails regardless of whether any gain or loss is involved. The risk/profit motive is lacking, and the disposition of economic control is incomplete.

Accounting Distinctions

As mentioned previously and depicted in Figure 1.2, certain investments generate income (or loss) during the period of holding. This income or loss has to be tax accounted for each year. This is an entirely separate accounting process from that which takes place at time of disposition. The consequence is that, for investments, there are TWO accounting processes. There is (1) income-while-holding accounting and (2) disposition accounting.

Income-while-holding accounting and disposition accounting are layman terms. More correctly, these processes are called *current* accounting and *capital* accounting, respectively. Confusion can — and often does — arise between these two processes.

The term "current" means within each taxable year, every year, while an asset is being held. If an investment asset is acquired during a taxable year (and it produces any income), current accounting starts with the acquisition date and continues through the end of the first taxable year: December 31. If an asset is disposed of during a taxable year, current accounting starts on January 1 of the disposition year and continues to the date of disposition. Otherwise, current accounting is required from January 1 through December 31 of each full holding year.

For capital accounting purposes, the term "capital" means money or money value, in dollars. Capital accounting spans the whole investment gamut from date of acquisition to date of disposition. It is the keeping track of the amount of money that initially went into the asset, plus any subsequent additions, less any subsequent withdrawals, plus or minus any tax adjustments, until disposition. Capital accounting is also called "tax basis" accounting. That is, one's *tax basis* in an asset is the reference base for determining one's gain or loss at time of disposition.

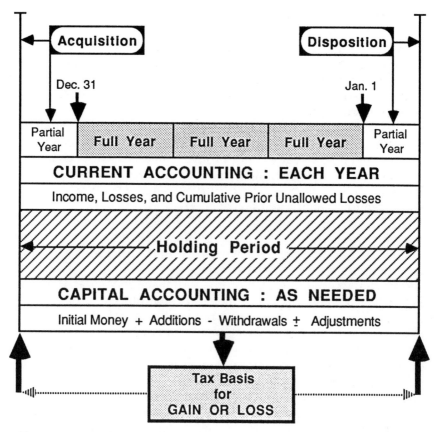

Fig. 1.3 - Distinction Between Current and Capital Accounting

A depiction of the concurrency — and distinction — between current accounting and capital accounting is presented in Figure 1.3. The longer the holding period, the greater the confusion and mixup of records between the two accounting methods.

When the time comes to sell an investment asset, many investors figure their gain or loss with reference to the acquisition cost only. They forget about the cost of additions, money withdrawals, depreciation deductions, and loss carryovers which have taken place during the holding period. The result, often, is that many investors pay higher taxes than they need to pay.

Flexibility of Choice

One of the true tax benefits of being an investor is that one can indeed control — to some extent — his own tax destiny. One can pick the year and manner of disposition that he wants. This is unlike tax-reportable ordinary income: salary, wages, interest, dividends, rents, royalties, etc.

An investor can select a disposition year which counterbalances his ordinary income. If he has a good capital gain, he can dispose of his asset(s) in a year of poor ordinary income. Or, if he has a net capital loss, he can institute disposition in a year of good ordinary income. There is much flexibility in what an investor can do, compared to a noninvestor taxpayer.

To participate in the opportunities of choice, one must advance a sum of money or other consideration for the acquisition of a capital asset. What is not so obvious is that the money or other consideration must be after-tax money or consideration. One cannot acquire an asset with pretax or tax-avoidance money and expect to get further tax benefits out of the use of that money. Consequently, the acquisition of a capital asset requires a "proof-of-basis" in that asset as well as "proof-of-ownership" thereof.

Ordinarily, an investor advances his money with the expectation of making a profit. Of course, there is no guarantee that he will do so. He enters the venture with the tacit understanding that there is some risk involved. He may make a profit (gain) or he may not. He must accept such risks as management decisions, market conditions, the general economy, government regulation, consumer lawsuits, labor strikes, and the like. Nevertheless, he must be primarily profit motivated.

At some point in time, an investor is one who makes the decision to dispose of the asset. He makes the decision irrespective of anyone else, other than co-owners. For such decision, a husband and wife are treated as one owner.

Disposition of an investment may be by sale, exchange, gift, inheritance, bankruptcy, theft, casualty, involuntary conversion, worthlessness, abandonment, and so on. The point here is that the form of disposition is irrelevant so long as the investor himself/herself makes the final decision, and he/she has the legal right to do so as the owner/holder.

2

COST WHEN SOLD

"Cost Or Other Basis" Is The Measure Of Money You Have In A Capital Asset When It Is Sold. Ordinarily, Purchase Cost Is The Initial Basis For Capital Accounting. However, For Non-Purchased Acquisitions, "Substituted Basis" Rules Apply. Once Acquired, There Are Various Adjustments To Basis (Plus And Minus): Capital-In, Capital-Out. There Is Also "Capitalization" Of Certain Holding Expenses And "Indexing" For Inflation For Long-Term Holdings. Upon Disposition, There Is "Return Of Capital" . . . Which Is Not Taxed.

Capital gain or loss occurs to an investor only when he sells an asset: not when he buys it. Until a sale or exchange — or other disposition — takes place, there is no way to fix the amount of gain or loss. Furthermore, it is the character of the asset at time of sale that determines whether it is a capital asset. The character may change between time of acquisition and time of disposition. Also, the cost may change.

The term "cost" means *cost or other basis* when property (in the form of a capital asset) is sold. The term "basis" means the amount of capital (money or money's worth) invested in that property. The term "sold" means sale, exchange, or other disposition. These terms, simple as they may sound, are extremely important to an investor. Ignoring the importance of simple terms can mean higher tax burdens than necessary.

For example, almost every investor knows what a "sale or exchange" is. But how many know what an "other disposition" is?

Not all transfers of property are effected by sale or exchange. There are many situations where property is conveyed for other than full and adequate consideration. Examples are gift, inheritance, theft, casualty, bankruptcy, abandonment, worthlessness, termination of a trust, dissolution of a partnership, liquidation of a corporation, involuntary conversion, government mandates, court-ordered transfers, and so on. All of these dispositions are treated as sales (or exchanges) for capital accounting purposes. If you ignore these dispositions, as many investors tend to do, you do so at your own tax peril.

Every transaction in property, that is, every capital asset that is disposed of, is reported to the IRS. (We will discuss this fully in the next chapter: Broker Reportings.) Since the IRS knows your gross sale proceeds, it will tax these proceeds as ordinary income unless you set forth your "cost or other basis" on your tax return.

In this chapter, therefore, we want to explain more fully those factors that establish your cost when an asset is sold. Establishing cost for tax purposes is not as simple as you may off-hand think. That is, if you want to pay minimum tax. If you want to pay maximum tax, then cost-when-sold is a simple matter. You simply assume zero cost, and pay tax on the gross proceeds.

Must "Capitalize" Costs, Etc.

As depicted back in Figure 1.1, a capital transaction consists of three phases. There is acquisition of the asset (Phase I); there is observation of it with the passage of time (Phase II); and there is disposition of it (Phase III). There is no capital accounting of the transaction until the asset is disposed of. The disposition may be by sale, exchange, or otherwise.

Because there is no capital accounting until sale of an asset, investors tend to get careless in their record-keeping duties. The longer the span of time between acquisition and disposition, the more inattentive and lethargic they become. The greater the number of transactions in a taxable year, the more troublesome and confusing the records become.

It is nice to make money on one's investments, and it is painful to lose it. It is even more painful (to some taxpayers) to keep proper records on each investment. Nevertheless, it is your duty to do so. The position of the IRS is this: If you do not keep complete records on *each transaction*, your gross proceeds (at time of sale) **is all gain**! You are maximum taxed accordingly.

On this point, we call your attention to Section 6001 of the Internal Revenue Code. It is headed: **Notice or regulations requiring records, statements, and special returns.** The phrase "special returns" means specific tax forms applicable to each taxpayer's own transactions.

In essential part, Section 6001 reads as follows:

Every person liable for any tax imposed . . . shall keep such records, render such statements, make such returns, and comply with such rules and regulations as the [IRS] *from time to time* [may] *prescribe. Whenever in the judgment of the* [IRS] *it is necessary,* [the IRS] *may require any person, by notice served upon such person or by regulations, . . . to keep such records . . .* [as are] *deemed sufficient to show whether or not such person is liable for tax.*

As an investor, you have no excuse. You are to keep *such records . . .* as are *necessary . . .* and *deemed sufficient.* We are not going to elaborate on your record-keeping requirements at this time. We'll do so as appropriate in later chapters.

All of which brings us to a very important tax-accounting point. All costs and expenses associated with an investment asset must be *capitalized.* That is, you must keep a running record of your costs *and* expenses as you go along. When expenses are capitalized, they add to the acquisition cost of the asset, to be subtracted from gross proceeds at time of sale. An illustration of what we are getting at here is presented in Figure 2.1.

The message in Figure 2.1 is that if you capitalize your costs and expenses properly, you can recover them at time of sale. The recovery is your "cost or other basis" in the asset sold. Your recovery also is *return of capital . . .* which is not taxed.

Dilemma With "Expenses"

As stressed in Chapter 1, the primary characteristic of an investor is passivity. But this description disturbs a lot of investors. They will argue vehemently that they do indeed actively manage their investments. They follow them every day; they maintain a separate office for doing so; they use computers and modems. Concerning their investments, they make phone calls, send mail, buy publications, buy software, pay fees and commissions, visit brokers and dealers, attend seminars, travel to stockholder meetings,

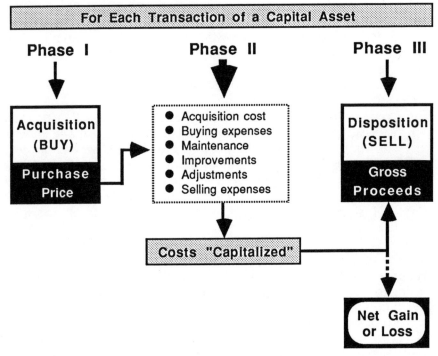

Fig. 2.1 - Capitalization of Costs Until Asset Disposition

and so on. All of these activities involve costs and expenses which they want to write off against their investments.

Yes, the above activities are certainly legitimate costs/expenses. But how do we handle them taxwise? Are they "costs," or are they "expenses"?

If they are "costs," they can be capitalized. No question about it. If they are "expenses," maybe they can be capitalized. But most likely not. If the asset (or group of assets) generate income, it is possible — indirectly — to write off some of the expenses against that income. It depends on the character of the asset(s) held.

On this expense-against-income point, Section 212: Expenses for Production of Income, says—

In the case of an individual, there shall be allowed as a deduction all the ordinary and necessary expenses paid or incurred during the taxable year—

(1) for the production or collection of income;
(2) for the management, conservation, or maintenance of property held for the production of income; or
(3) in connection with the determination, collection, or refund of any tax.

This all sounds great . . . until you read Section 67(a): the 2% AGI rule (AGI is "adjusted gross income"). Section 67(a) reads in part—

In the case of an individual, the miscellaneous itemized deductions for any taxable year shall be allowed only to the extent that the aggregate of such deductions exceeds 2 percent of adjusted gross income.

In other words, all self-management-type investment expenses (except for rental and royalty income property) are treated as miscellaneous itemized deductions on your annual income tax return. Thus, until your current investment expenses exceed 2% of your adjusted gross income — from all sources — you get no tax writeoff whatsoever. Section 67(a) pretty well rules out Section 212-type expenses for maintaining and directing one's own investments.

This is some respite from the 2% AGI rule if any of the expenses can be legitimately characterized as *carrying charges*. The tax law on point is Section 266: Election to Capitalize Carrying Charges. The regulations thereunder, however, restrict carrying charges to such items as taxes (property, transfer, excise), interest, insurance, freight, and other capitalizable-type costs.

Essential Characteristics

Knowing what costs and expenses to capitalize is *the* prerequisite for good records for tax basis purposes. Helpful in this regard is a definitive explanation of the characteristics of an investment capital asset. There are five such characteristics, namely:

1. Property or rights to property;
2. Owned (or co-owned) by the taxpayer;
3. Held primarily for investment;
4. Value ascertainable at time of acquisition; and
5. Value ascertainable at time of disposition.

A capital asset must be property in some form. It can be the physical item itself, such as equipment, vehicle, building, land, gold, patent, territory, or whatever. It also can be *rights* to the physical item or items. Rights to property are usually fractional interests in the form of shares, options, leases, franchises, contracts, and so on. Behind the legal documentation of property rights, there must be physical property of some specific tangible form. If there are neither property nor rights to property in some manner, the transaction is a sham. There is nothing to which to attach value.

A capital asset must be owned and held by the taxpayer filing an income tax return. The taxpayer must be the clear legal owner of that portion which he claims/reports as his asset. If it is owned by some other person or some entity other than the filing taxpayer, it is not a capital asset for tax benefits. Ownership must be legal physical possession, or legal dominion and control, or legal title holder in the state where the property or rights to property are acquired. Stolen property, for example, cannot be sold or exchanged for the tax benefits of a capital asset.

A capital asset must be held primarily for investment. This does not mean exclusively, so long as other uses are de minimis in amount. The asset may experience some — very limited — personal use, business use, subdivision use, and even some active participation (management) by the owner. But, by and large, the asset must be held primarily for investment purposes, rather than for personal or business use. There are specific tax reasons for this.

A capital asset must have ascertainable value at the time of its acquisition. If it has no value whatsoever, it is not property or rights to property. Having ascertainable value means that the taxpayer or someone else is willing to pay or trade for it, when not under compulsion to do so. Ordinarily, value generally means $1 or more. However, so-called "penny stock" has value if that is all someone is willing to pay for it, and the stock does indeed have some physical assets behind it worth $1 or more. In special circumstances, a physical item of property could have zero value, so long as immediately after acquisition a necessary improvement is made to give it a finite value. The value at time of acquisition becomes the initial reference for determining any gain or loss upon disposition.

A capital asset also must have ascertainable value at the time of its disposition. In this case, it could have zero value so long as it can be truly ascertained to be zero. The term "zero" is a specific numerical value which is not negative. However, if property has zero value upon acquisition, it cannot have zero value upon disposition. There must be some *change in value* during the period of holding by the taxpayer.

Indeed, the basic ingredient of any capital asset is that there be a change in value with the passing of time. It may appreciate in value, in which case there is capital gain. Or, it may decline in value, in which case there is capital loss. Lacking this underlying ingredient, an asset becomes noncapital. For example, any form of promise or guarantee of return of initial capital cannot be a capital asset. That is, assuming that the initial capital — no more, no less — is indeed returned. Otherwise, there must be some risk of variation between initial and final values.

To emphasize the above, we show in Figure 2.2 the three ownership phases of a capital asset. In each of these phases, there are certain costs and expenses which can be — and should be — capitalized. As the investor, therefore, it is your job to allocate your costs and expenses properly. You can best do this by identifying them with the specific characteristics enumerated above.

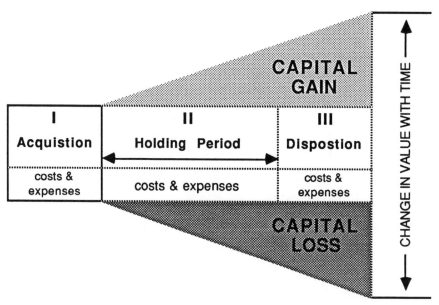

Fig. 2.2 - Ownership Phases for Identifying Capital Costs

Cost as (Initial) Basis

The ordinary concept of "cost" is deceptive. It is the amount paid for property in cash, promises, services, and other property. What is allowable as cost for tax purposes may differ significantly from what one thinks of as cost.

The very first requirement of cost is that the property be acquired through an *arm's-length purchase*. The amount, form, and time of payment are irrelevant. Whether the buyer paid more or less than it is worth is not of tax concern. There is no adjustment to cost for bad bargains or good bargains, so long as the agreed price is above-board between unrelated and unconniving seller and buyer.

If property is bought on credit and/or with borrowed funds, cost is the full purchase price plus associated loan costs. Associated costs include loan application fees, customary "points," broker commissions, refinance charges, appraisal fees, title searches, inspections and permits, and so on. All costs of borrowing money, establishing credit, and acquiring title are properly includible in initial cost basis, so long as there is full legal obligation on the acquirer to repay the borrowed funds.

If property is purchased at an arm's-length price, together with an agreement by the buyer to assume the seller's or third-party's debt obligations against that property, cost includes all debt obligations assumed. That is, mortgage debt, promissory notes, contract debts, tax liens, mechanics liens, and other debt encumbrances assumed by the buyer, and enforceable upon him, are properly includible in his cost.

When there are exchanges of debt obligations between seller and buyer, there is misunderstanding of what constitutes the cost element thereof. For example, consider that the seller has a $15,000 debt obligation which the buyer takes over, and the buyer has a $10,000 debt obligation which the seller takes over. What is the "cost" portion to the buyer?

It is $5,000. The buyer assumed a debt of $15,000 and was relieved of a debt of $10,000. Debt assumed minus debt relieved is "cost." If the other way around (debt relief greater than debt assumed), the cost is reduced accordingly.

In a nutshell, one's initial cost consists of all elements necessary to acquire legal title to property. In addition to purchase price, it includes search expenses, advisory fees, attorney fees, advertising expenses, appraisal fees, broker commissions, title fees, transfer taxes, certification fees, certified mail, phone . . . the whole works.

Whatever it costs you to buy the asset — from "day one" to the date you receive legal title in hand — is your acquisition cost. You can capitalize 100% of these costs and expenses.

When Not at Arm's Length

Ordinarily, in a bona fide sale, the cost to the buyer (purchaser) is the fair market value to the seller. This is the premise upon which the market value theory is based. The seller is profit motivated and seeking the best deal that he can get. The buyer is also profit motivated in seeking the best investment he can get. Prior to the sell-buy transaction, neither the seller nor buyer is obligated to each other nor related in any way. The resulting cost is purely at arm's length, called "fair market value."

Where other than pure economic motives are present, the cost-as-basis rule is modified. If the price paid is more than its fair market value, the cost is fair market value on date of acquisition. If the price paid is less than fair market value, cost is the lower amount paid. This is the non-arm's-length rule which says the acquirer's cost basis is his actual cost or fair market value . . . *whichever is lower*.

This "whichever lower" rule is not so clearly stated in the federal tax code. Instead, it is judicial precedent evolving from many Tax Court cases where the IRS has asserted its "presumption of gift" theory. The presumption is that if property is purchased at a cost other than fair market value, there must have been a gift involved. Whether this presumption is true or not is another matter. It certainly raises many questions.

For example, why would one sell for $10,000 a capital asset clearly worth $50,000? Has the seller made a gift of $40,000 to the buyer? If so, what are the personal, special, financial, and underground relationships involved?

Conversely, why would a buyer pay $50,000 for a capital asset clearly worth only $10,000? Has the buyer made a gift of $40,000 to the seller? If so, what are the facts and circumstances involved?

In Figure 2.3, an attempt is made to depict the whichever-lower rule: purchase cost or fair market value. Note the heavy horizontal line labeled "At Arm's Length." Note also the horizontal shaded zone. The shading represents a reasonable band of haggling tolerance between seller and buyer. That portion of price outside of this haggling zone is deemed to be a gift.

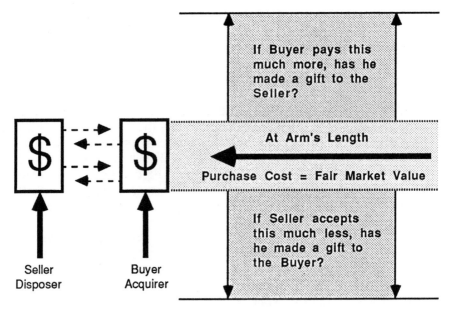

Fig. 2.3 - Concept of Arm's-Length Cost as Initial Basis

"Whichever is lower at time of acquisition" means that the taxable gain at time of disposition will be higher than the taxpayer anticipated. It also means that the recognized loss at time of disposition will be less than the taxpayer anticipated. Thus, the whichever-lower rule is definitely a disadvantage. The disadvantage is purposely set. It puts the taxpayer on notice to prove his basis.

Zero Basis Presumption

If one wants the tax benefits of capital gain/capital loss, he is expected to prove the cost of his purchased property. He must keep such records and provide such facts and statements as necessary to establish his basis in *each separate* capital asset acquired. This burden of proof on the taxpayer is a principle of long standing. Failure to prove cost can result in a zero basis for the property.

Initial cost is only part of the equation. As you'll see subsequently, the initial cost itself — "as adjusted" — can change with time. It is for this change-in-cost reason that the tax term *cost or other basis* is used. This term or its equivalent appears on the tax forms when reporting your capital transactions. Obviously, you are expected to prove your initial cost plus any other basis adjustments you might make. Thus, it is particularly important that you have and retain your acquisition cost documents. Your cost basis has to have a provable starting point.

Consequently, if you have no cost records on your acquisitions, you are in for a difficult time. Without records, the tax presumption is that your acquisition basis is zero. This, of course, maximizes your tax if you dispose of property at a gain. If you dispose of property at what you think is a loss, zero basis means that the loss is not tax recognized.

The zero basis presumption by the IRS is strictly arbitrary. It is the hair-thread premise on which your burden of proof emanates. The IRS presumes that if you have no records of purchase cost, you either acquired the asset illegally, or it was given to you underhandedly by some family member who wanted to avoid paying tax on it. Thus, the zero basis presumption has some validity for tax enforcement purposes.

"Minimum Evidence" Rule

The zero-basis presumption can be overridden by the rule of "minimum evidence." This rule requires that *any evidence* that has a material and factual relationship to the property acquired can be used to establish its cost-or-other basis. The evidence must relate in some manner to the property in question, and it must provide some factual cost foundation on which basis information can be derived. One's testimony alone is insufficient.

For example, consider a taxpayer who, over a period of several years, bought a number of gold coins. On each purchase he paid cash (in green paper) because that is what the coin dealer wanted. The coin dealer had been stuck with bad checks in the past. He also had many lawsuits over price quotations (which fluctuate hourly). Furthermore, the coin dealer had been burglarized and his sales records to customers stolen. The burglars used the records to burglarize his customers, which produced further lawsuits against him. He wanted cash only. So, prior to each purchase of coins, the taxpayer went to his savings bank and withdrew an approximate amount of money.

Subsequently, the taxpayer sold the coins in one bulk lot. The coin dealer paid with a business check, which the taxpayer promptly deposited. No purchase or sales slips were ever provided by the coin dealer. What is the acquisition cost or other basis in the coins in this case?

First, the taxpayer has to establish the number of coins sold. If not the number of coins, the number of ounces of gold that were sold. Since gold is an international commodity, the daily bid-ask price can be found in authoritative financial journals. The taxpayer photocopies the market quotes corresponding to the date of deposit of his sale proceeds. From the published unit prices on gold, the whole number of coins or ounces can be determined.

Next, the taxpayer has to dig back into reference files (such as at a public library) on financial journals which quote the price of gold. For each date of his withdrawal from savings, he makes a photocopy of the relevant financial journal. He matches up the unit prices (ounces or coins) in the nearest whole numbers to each of his withdrawal amounts. By trial and error, the total number of ounces or coins in his separate purchases must equal the number he sold.

His acquisition basis then is the number of coins purchased each date of savings withdrawal, times the unit market price quoted on that date. Since the published prices are wholesale (not retail at which he bought), his "other basis" will be lower than his actual cost. So he pays more tax than he would have had he kept accurate cost records.

The above example is purposely detailed. It illustrates the pain and effort required to satisfactorily override the zero basis tax presumption. The moral is obvious. Each taxpayer must keep his own cost records on his own acquisitions. He cannot rely on others to do it for him.

Basis Upon Exchange

In the world of capital assets, exchanges of property or rights to property are common occurrences. Exchanges minimize the amount of cash that changes hands. They allow swapping of property forms, debt obligations, and ownership responsibilities. Depending on the circumstances, exchanges may be taxable or nontaxable.

In a taxable exchange, an owner gives up property worth some value determined by general market conditions. In its place he acquires other property of unlike kind, but of equivalent value. If he reports and pays tax on the transaction, his basis in the property acquired in the exchange is its market value. This is so even if no cash changes hands.

Consider, for example, that owner A had a parcel of land with a cost basis of $10,000. The land is worth $25,000. Owner B wants the land but does not have any cash. He offers A marketable stock and securities worth $25,000. Owner A accepts the stock and securities and conveys to B title to the land. Owner A pays tax on the difference between $25,000 and his $10,000 basis. When he does so, his basis in the new property (stock and securities) is $25,000.

A so-called "nontaxable" exchange is really a misnomer. It is true that at the moment of exchange there is no tax. But at some event downstream, there will be a tax. More appropriately, the term "tax-deferred" applies. Somewhere along the line, a capital transaction will be involved, and tax will apply. You can count on it . . . years later.

All tax-deferred exchanges have a common ingredient. The primary properties exchanged are *like in kind*. That is, they are "tax like" in kind. For example, raw land for similar land, productive equipment for productive equipment, livestock for livestock (of same sex), commercial diamonds for commercial diamonds, and so on. No gain or loss is recognized (for tax purposes) in like-kind exchanges.

The tax law on point is Section 1031(a). This section, subheaded as **Exchanges solely in kind**, reads in part as:

*No gain or loss shall be recognized if property held for productive use in trade or business **or for investment** . . . is exchanged solely for property **of a like kind** to be held either for productive use in trade or business or for investment.* [Emphasis added.]

Section 1031(a) says that a like-kind exchange is nontaxable. It says nothing about basis in the property acquired in the exchange. Section 1031(d) addresses this point. In pertinent part, this subsection reads—

If property was acquired on an exchange described in this section . . . then the basis shall be the same as that of the property exchanged, decreased in the amount of any money received by the taxpayer and increased by the amount of gain . . . that was recognized on such exchange.

In other words, in a like-kind exchange, one's basis is simply *transferred* from his old property to his new property, plus or minus certain adjustments. Many taxpayers/investors miss this point altogether. They think that if they acquire property worth $25,000 in exchange for property with a basis of $10,000, their new basis is $25,000. This is incorrect. They merely transfer their old basis to the new, which is $10,000.

Gifts and Inheritances

Apart from purchases and exchanges, property may be acquired by gift. In a bona fide gift, full title to property is conveyed from the giver (called: *donor*) to the receiver (called: *donee*) exactly as though a sale or exchange had taken place. The only difference is that no money or money's worth is paid.

The gifting of a single asset may occur in one of three general forms. The transfer may be a full gift 100%. It may be part gift and part sale. Or, it may be part gift and part retention, such as in a life estate. Whichever form is involved, it is the gifted portion whose basis upon acquisition must be ascertained.

There is a special rule for determining one's basis in property acquired by gift. It is embodied in Section 1015 of the Internal Revenue Code. It is a complicated rule. The gist is that basis in the hands of the donee is—

    (1)   the donor's adjusted basis
         OR
    (2)   the fair market value

   . . . **whichever is lower**.

Usually, but not always, the donor's adjusted basis is lower. This is particularly so if appreciated property is given. The donor's adjusted basis is his acquisition cost, plus additions, less subtractions. Since most donors don't keep track of their tax basis, they leave it up to the donee.

Property also may be acquired by inheritance. After all of the legal change of ownership and probative aspects are out of the way, the property gets a "new start" tax basis. Generally, the new start is the fair market value of the property on one of three valuation dates.

The new start dates are prescribed by Section 1014 of the tax code. This section is headed: **Basis of property acquired from a decedent**. It reads in part as follows:

Except as otherwise provided in this section, the basis of property in the hands of a person acquiring the property from a decedent or to whom the property passed from a decedent shall, if not sold, exchanged, or otherwise disposed of before the decedent's death by such person, be—
(1) the fair market value of the property at the date of the decedent's death, or
(2) . . . its value at the applicable valuation date prescribed by [Section 2032 . . . within and up to 6 months after the decedent's death], *or*
(3) . . . its value determined under [Section 2032A . . . relating to qualified real property used in farming or other trade or business during the 8-year period ending on the date of the decedent's death].

As you might surmise from the above, basiswise, acquisition by inheritance is more tax favorable than acquisition by gift. Property acquired from a decedent is treated as though it were purchased from the decedent at its market value. In contrast, property acquired by gift involves a transfer of basis (much like an exchange), with "adjustments" thereto.

Substituted Basis Rules

Special — and often complex — basis rules apply to the acquisition of property other than by purchase, exchange, gift, or inheritance. There indeed are many other acquisition situations involving property held for investment. They are simply too numerous to attempt to discuss them here in any meaningful way.

The general premise on which the special basis rules apply is the *substituted* basis concept. The "substitution" of basis is characterized by two approaches, namely—

(1) by reference to the basis in the hands of a transferor, donor, or grantor, or
(2) by reference to other property held at any time by the person from whom the basis is to be determined.

These two approaches are embodied in the wording of Section 1016(b): **Substituted basis**. This subsection reads in full as—

Whenever it appears that the basis of property in the hands of the taxpayer is a substituted basis, then the adjustments provided in subsection (a) shall be made after first making in respect of such substituted basis proper adjustments of a similar nature in respect of the period during which the property was held by the transferor, donor, or grantor, or during which the other property was held by the person for whom the basis is to be determined. A similar rule shall be applied in the case of a series of substituted bases.

The referenced "subsection (a)" consists of 25 adjustment possibilities! Each of these 25 adjustments is set forth in a separate subsection of its own. This is just one rule: Section 1016.

Altogether, there are some 38 basis rules, including Section 1016. Among these 38 are Sections 307 (Basis of distributed stock and stock rights), 723 (Basis of property contributed to partnership), 1017 (Basis upon discharge of indebtedness), 1041 (Basis of property transferred in divorce), 1056 (Basis for player contracts in a franchise), . . . and many others. All of these basis rules involve particular adjustments and substitution concepts.

When property is acquired on a substituted basis, the basis just prior to the acquisition is the "adjusted basis" in the hands of the prior holder. After acquisition, the new holder starts his basis accounting as though the property were a *continuation* of the prior holder's basis. Thereafter, subsequent adjustments are made for additions and subtractions, just as though the property had been purchased. If the acquirer pays any brokerage fees, and/or transfer or exchange costs, these add to the basis of the property acquired.

The substitution concept is of fundamental importance to those transactions where no consideration at all is paid, or where the consideration is substantially less than the fair market value of the property received. The concept applies also to a *series* of substituted bases.

An attempt to illustrate this important concept is presented in Figure 2.4. Note that there are two prior holders "A" and "B." The present holder of the property is "C." The present holder picks up the basis transfers from "A" and "B," as his initial basis. To "C's" initial basis there are "adjustments" that he himself makes.

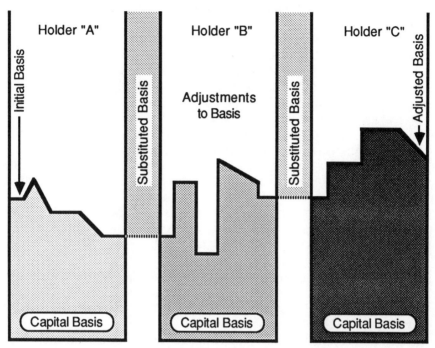

Fig. 2.4 - Concept of Substituted Basis for Nonpurchased Assets

Adjustments to Basis

When one acquires a capital asset by purchase or otherwise, his initial basis is not forever cast in concrete. Throughout the period of holding the asset, there are likely to be various adjustments to basis. Some of the adjustments will reflect the doings of others.

As in any accounting process, adjustments are made in two directions: plus and minus. Plus adjustments are additions to basis; minus adjustments are subtractions from basis. Upon disposition of the asset, one has an "adjusted basis."

As an everyday illustration of additions to basis, consider shares in a mutual stock fund with "automatic reinvestment" privileges. Periodically, management of the fund makes distributions from its profits and other transactions. Distributions are in the form of dividends, capital gains, and nontaxable refunds. These distributions are reportable each year on the income tax returns of each individual investor. The distributions are automatically reinvested by management.

Except for endless reams of computer printouts sent by management, the investor never sees the reinvested distributions. As a consequence, when the shares are sold, many investors fail to add the automatic reinvestments to their initial basis. They report more gain and less loss than they need to. The end result: they tax themselves twice on the reinvested money!

Other additions to basis include capital improvements, commissions, freight (shipping or postage), storage costs, renovations, defense of title, refinance costs, and other investor outlays to upgrade and ready his capital asset for arm's-length disposition.

There are also subtractions from basis. Subtractions are "return of capital." They are recoveries of invested money through partial sales, lawsuit awards, insurance proceeds, nontaxable dividends, seller refunds, tax credits, and so on.

Government is alert and ever-ready to subtract from basis certain allowable income tax credits and deductions. Examples are amortization, depletion, depreciation, subsidy payments, energy credits, and other tax benefits.

The cancellation or reduction of indebtedness, other than customary paybacks, is treated as subtraction from basis. The subtraction applies only to reduction of original debt made by the seller, or in bankruptcy proceedings, or due to unmaterialized contingencies. A special law — Section 1017: Discharge of Indebtedness — addresses this subject. Since the original debt is part of one's initial basis in property, any discharge of that debt through forgiveness is a reduction in basis.

The Reality of Inflation

If one invests his money in a capital asset, he is entitled to "return of his capital" before any tax applies. Ideally, one would like to get back dollars with the same purchasing power as when he initially invested. In reality, we know that this does not happen. Dollars invested 10 years ago, if returned in full to the penny, will have depreciated in value. We all know this.

Consider raw, undeveloped land, for example. It has inherent value based on its geographic location, its subsurface minerals, its surface nutrients, and its above-surface access to sun and rain. If the raw land sits from year to year, and is not developed, its value will not have changed. Yet, the number of dollars required to buy it will change from year to year. Why? Because of inflation.

Depreciation of the dollar is recognized in Social Security benefits, government wages and salaries, and Congressional and Judicial salaries and pensions. In private businesses, price adjustments for inflation are regularly made. In labor contracts and nonunion wage scales, cost-of-living adjustments are made (more or less) annually. In these and other monetary transactions, the number of dollars involved is indexed to inflation. In view of these realities, it is totally unrealistic to ignore inflation adjustments to invested capital.

The nearest authorization for indexing return of capital is found in Section 1016(a)(1): **Adjustments to basis: General rule.** The introductory part of this section reads as—

Proper adjustment in respect of the property shall in all cases be made . . . for expenditures, receipts, losses, or other items, properly chargeable to capital account. . . .

The phrase "or other items, properly chargeable to capital account" would certainly include monetary inflation. The problem is that there is no administratively approved procedure for inflation adjustments to capital investments. Consequently, one seeking to do so must lay a proper and convincing foundation on an asset-by-asset basis.

Tiptoeing to Indexation

The first glimmer of statutory recognition of inflation indexing for tax matters came in 1981. On June 26, 1981 the U.S. Senate Committee on Finance issued Press Release No. 81-21. On page 11 thereof, the announcement stated that—

. . . The individual tax rate brackets, personal exemption, and zero bracket amount would be adjusted for inflation, beginning on January 1, 1985. . . . Accordingly, the adjustment . . . would be based on the Consumer Price Index for fiscal year 1984. . . . Similar adjustments would be made in the tax tables for each subsequent taxable year.

This press release was subsequently followed by an amendment to Section 1 of the Internal Revenue Code. Subsection (f) was added. This new subsection 1(f) is officially headed: **Adjustments in tax tables so that inflation will not result in tax increases**. One could *imply* that similar adjustments could be made to one's capital basis. But this is an implication only. Section 1(f) applies specifically to tax rates: not to invested capital.

On May 29, 1985, the President released his proposals to Congress for "Fairness, Growth, and Simplicity" in taxes. On page 166 of his 460-page proposal, the concepts above were applied to investment capital. The relevant wording on point was—

> *Because the preferential tax rate (for long-term capital gain) does not account systematically for the effects of inflation, investors face substantial uncertainty regarding the eventual effective rate of tax on their investments, and may even be taxed on investments that produce an economic loss. The availability to investors of an election to index the basis of capital assets, in lieu of a preferential rate, would reduce uncertainty over effective tax rates and ensure only that real gains are subject to tax.*

Although the capital gain indexing proposal in 1985 never became law, Congress in 1986 did index the cost basis of automobiles used in a trade or business. The recognition of reality was set forth in tax code Section 280F(d)(7): **Automobile price inflation adjustment**. Affected taxpayers were specifically directed to use the Consumer Price Index (CPI) data published by government.

Based on the above, the idea of indexing invested capital has been portrayed as a valid adjustment for tax purposes. The express statutory details for doing so have yet to be promulgated.

Use of CPI Data

In order to make capital adjustments for inflation, one needs official CPI information. The government agency responsible for publishing CPI's each year (monthly) is the Bureau of Labor Statistics in the Department of Labor. For historical purposes, CPI indexes for the 30-year period 1961-1990 are presented in Figure 2.5. Current-year indexes can be obtained from various financial periodicals and publications.

Inflation adjustment (indexing) of one's cost basis is done on the date of disposition of the capital asset. A *multiplying factor* is

YEAR	CPI	YEAR	CPI
1961	89.6	1976	174.3
1962	90.6	1977	185.4
1963	91.7	1978	204.9
1964	92.9	1979	220.7
1965	94.5	1980	248.1
1966	97.2	1981	272.4
1967	100.0	1982	289.1
1968	104.2	1983	294.4
1969	109.8	1984	311.1
1970	116.3	1985	322.2
1971	121.3	1986	328.4
1972	125.3	1987	340.4
1973	133.1	1988	354.3
1974	147.7	1989	372.9
1975	161.2	1990	398.8

* Data From U.S. Department of Labor, Bureau of Labor Statistics
U.S. City Average, All Urban Consumers.

Fig. 2.5 - 30-Year Period of Consumer Price Indexes

involved. This multiplier is the ratio of the CPI for year of disposition to the CPI for the year of acquisition. In other words,

$$\text{Inflation adjustment to capital basis} = \frac{\text{CPI year of disposition}}{\text{CPI year of acquisition}}$$

Let us illustrate with a numerical example. Consider a capital asset acquired in 1980 and disposed of in 1990. Assume that its cost basis on date of acquisition was $10,000. Upon indexing, its revised basis would be

$$\$10,000 \times \frac{398.8 \text{ (CPI for 1990)}}{248.1 \text{ (CPI for 1980)}} = \$10,000 \times 1.6074$$

$$= \$16,074$$

Thus, instead of one's return of capital being $10,000 "as acquired," it would be $16,074 "as indexed." This is a much more equitable return of capital. There is no "inflation tax" on the $6,074 ($16,074 - $10,000).

Do Your Homework

To claim the adjustment-to-cost basis for monetary inflation, you are cautioned to do your homework properly. Do not try to index for every dollar that you add to your investment (after acquisition) nor for every dollar that you remove from your investment (before disposition). This complicates matters too much. Establish your cost or other basis as adjusted, *before* applying the inflation factor. For simplicity, use the CPI's for year of acquisition and year of disposition only.

Let us expand on the $10,000 illustration above (same acquisition year, same disposition year). Suppose you added $3,500 to your investment during the course of time of your holding it. Suppose you received a $1,800 nontaxable distribution from it. And, suppose your out-of-pocket (documented) holding expenses were $750. What would be your cost basis upon indexing?

Answer:

$$[\$10,000 + 3,500 - 1,800 + 750] \times 1.6074 = \$20,012$$

The figure $20,012 is what you enter into the appropriate column of your tax return as your *cost or other basis*. There is no way the IRS computer can check this figure. Consequently, you are on your own. This is why we caution you to do your homework properly, in case the IRS should question you.

There are other cautions, too. Do not attempt to inflation index for holding period less than one year. It takes about a year before the CPI figures are confirmed and officially published. For holding periods more than one year but less than five years, use official quarterly CPI's nearest to your dates of acquisition/disposition. For holding periods more than five years, use the end-of-year CPI's. Always photocopy the CPI data that you use, and attach it to your working papers supporting the computations on your tax return.

The amount you enter as cost-or-other basis is *return of capital*. It is not taxed!

Because return of capital is not taxed, it is incumbent upon each asset holder to establish his cost basis with certainty. An accounting for one's initial basis, together with applicable adjustments thereto, is the best assurance of this certainty.

3

BROKER REPORTINGS

TEFRA '82 Mandated A Whole New Tax Game In Capital Transactions. Starting Then, All Brokers, Middlemen, And Overseers Must Report To The IRS — On Forms 1099-A, 1099-B, 1099-S, And Schedules K-1 — All Sales, Exchanges, And Other Dispositions Of Investment Assets. The Gross Proceeds Must Be Reported For "Computer Matching": That IRS Dream For Total Control Over Investors. Reported Losses, Deductions, And Credits Are Computer Ignored. Recalcitrant Investors Are Subject To 20% Backup Withholding Plus Full Tax On The Gross Proceeds.

We live in a brutal tax world. All brokers, financial institutions, barter exchangers, realty agents, and other intermediaries must report all capital transactions to the IRS. Each and every separate transaction — sale, exchange, or other transfer of a capital asset — must be reported. Severe penalties are imposed on brokers for not doing so.

There are a few exceptions to the broker-reporting mandate. But, by and large, gone are the days when each individual taxpayer reported his capital transactions on his own. Big Brother now is reaching for near-absolute control over all property and assets owned by private individuals. The reach is choke-tight. It's all done through computer access by the IRS to our bank, broker, and other financial accounts.

Back in the 16th century, in monarchical Europe, revenue collections were made by "tax farming." Tax farmers were private entrepreneurs, commissioned by the reigning monarchs, to go out into the lands to force-collect revenue at whatever rates the traffic could bear. Out of this, there arose the practice of chain-whipping taxpayers to get them to report their sources of sustenance. Since then, tax revolutions have come and gone. But tax farming in the U.S. still persists.

Today, tax farming is performed by private brokers, etc. reporting on their own customers and clients. The world's most sophisticated tax-reporting system got started in earnest in 1982.

Birth of the Chokehold

On September 3, 1982, the **Tax Equity and Fiscal Responsibility Act** was enacted into law. This Act of Congress was heralded as a "revenue enhancement" and "tax punishment" measure. For acronymic reference, the letters T-E-F-R-A are most commonly used.

The basic idea behind TEFRA is to enhance taxpayer compliance. By so doing, more revenue will gush into the bottomless pit of the federal coffers. Anyone who protests frivolously on his tax return the compliance procedures can be fined $500 . . . "in addition to any other penalty provided by law." [Code Sec. 6702.]

Among TEFRA's 200 added provisions of tax law, vigorous new reporting rules were enacted. Most pertinent to our coverage in this book is the TEFRA section on "Broker Transactions Reports." The Act defines in broad terms who a broker is, for information reporting purposes. It gives the IRS additional powers to require reporting the *gross proceeds* on every sale or exchange executed for a customer. Of particular interest to us are the two TEFRA definitions of a broker and a customer.

TEFRA defines a "broker" as—

Any person who (for a consideration) regularly acts as a middleman with respect to property or services.

This encompasses anyone and everyone in the business world who performs a brokerage-type service for a commission or fee. This includes stock brokers, bond dealers, neighborhood bankers, savings institutions, real estate agents, mortgage lenders, title companies, account executives, financial advisers, mutual fund managers, insurance adjusters, coin exchangers, barter arrangers, commodity traders, futures contractors, and the like. This broker definition is all-sweeping.

TEFRA defines a "customer" as—

Any person for whom a broker has transacted any business.

The term "any business" means a brokerage transaction involving: (a) transfer of property, (b) redemption of securities, (c) retirement of indebtedness, or (d) closing a transaction (in commodities, personal property, or real property). So if one pays a commission or fee for selling, exchanging, or otherwise transferring any capital asset, he/she is a "customer" of a broker.

TEFRA goes on to require that every customer must supply to a broker his/her own Social Security number. The number must be provided every time a capital transaction is executed. If there were 20 capital transactions in a given year, for example, the customer would have to furnish his/her Social Security number 20 times for that year. A customer who fails to do so is subject to a $50 penalty . . . for each failure.

Brokers, too, are subject to the TEFRA penalty. If a broker fails to file an information return with the IRS for each transaction that he executes for a customer, he can be penalized $50 for each such failure. Furthermore, he can be penalized up to $100,000 for cumulative failures in any calendar year. If he intentionally disregards the reporting rules of TEFRA, he can be penalized 5% of the gross proceeds that he transacts, without limit. This could pretty well wipe out his entire brokerage commissions every year.

Code Section 6045

The statutory force for reporting all capital transactions is embodied in Section 6045 of the Internal Revenue Code. This section is captioned: **Returns of brokers.**

This is a good example of misleading captions in tax law. Section 6045 does not pertain to the personal income tax returns of brokers themselves. Instead, it prescribes *information returns* to be submitted by brokers. Thus, a more appropriate caption would have been: Information Returns by Brokers (not "of").

Section 6045(a) prescribes the general reporting mandate. It is sufficiently important to our discussion that we quote it in full. It reads—

Every person doing business as a broker shall, when required by the Secretary, make a return, in accordance with such regulations as the Secretary may prescribe, showing the name and address of each customer, with such details regarding gross proceeds and such other information as the Secretary may by forms or regulations require with respect to such business.

Section 6045(a) comprises a total of 58 words. (Count them yourself.) But look at the power placed in the person of the Secretary. The term "Secretary" means the Secretary of the Treasury or his delegate. The delegate of interest to us is the Commissioner of Internal Revenue.

The IRS Commissioner is appointed to office by each elected President. If the appointee happens to be a reasonable person, his regulations may be reasonable. But if he loves and thrives on executive power — as many in government do — his regulations can be tyrannical. We contend that Section 6045(a) allocates entirely too much discretionary power to one person. There are dangerous implications and precedents here. Our cherished democratic principles are in jeopardy.

There is one constructive note, however. Reporting under Section 6045(a) is only required where regulations are so prescribed "with respect to such business." This means that if the IRS forms and regulations are not clear and specific, a broker has some options in not reporting every ordinary transaction.

Regulation 1.6045-1

On November 15, 1982, the Commissioner of Internal Revenue issued his first regulations under Section 6045. In his explanatory background, he stated (among other things) that—

Brokers would be required to report the gross proceeds on all sales (including short sales) of securities and commodities and closing transactions in forward contracts affected for customers that occur during the broker's reporting period. . . . The regulations require reports with respect to each transaction and require the use of magnetic media because alternative methods of reporting provide information in an unusable form and would not result in the improved compliance contemplated by Congress. . . . The proposed regulations permit brokers to elect a monthly, quarterly, or annual reporting period. Brokers may send statements to their customers on the same basis.

The Commissioner then set forth in detail his requirements identified as Regulation 1.6045-1. He alone concluded that the effective date for IRS enforcement would be July 1, 1983.

Regulation 1.6045-1, as initially promulgated, consisted of "just" 6,000 words. By 1990, the regulatory wording had grown to 13,500! True to form, a bureaucratic monster has been created. Poor Congress. It doesn't know how to get the monster back in the cage.

Regulation 1.6045-1 is officially titled: **Returns of Information of brokers and barter exchanges**. It is much too extensive for a complete discussion here.

Despite the extensiveness of Regulation 1.6045-1, at least one selected excerpt is instructive. Consider the term "gross proceeds," for example. Regulation 1.6045-1(d)(5) specifically says—

The gross proceeds on a sale are the total amount paid to the customer or credited to the customer's account as a result of such sale.

Now, for the practical effect. Suppose a customer buys a 5-year Treasury Bond for $10,000. After a year or so, he sells the bond through a broker for $9,765. He has a capital *loss* of $235. Is there any federal tax revenue to be gained on the $235 loss? Of course not. Then, why does the broker have to report the $9,765 gross proceeds?

It is not just the $50 penalty revenue that your government wants. There is a more insidious reason. It is called "backup withholding."

Backup Withholding: 20%

TEFRA introduced a whole new concept in federal tax administration. It set forth a punitive procedure called *backup withholding*. Starting in 1984, a backup withholding amount equal to 20% of gross proceeds can be imposed. This is for not reporting on one's return his gross sale proceeds, even when a capital loss is sustained.

This punitive power was granted to the IRS by a whole new section of the tax code, namely, Section 3406: **B a c k u p**

withholding. This section consists of nine subsections, 36 sub-subsections, comprising approximately 4,000 words of tax law. The essence of relevance here is—

> *In the case of any reportable payment ... (relating to returns of brokers) ... if the payee fails to furnish his* [Social Security number], *or ...* [underreports his transactions] *... the payer shall deduct and withhold from such payment a tax equal to 20 percent of such payment.*

The 20% backup withholding power applies also to other than informational returns of brokers. But such other applications are beyond our concern. It is important that we be aware that, for the first time in the history of this Nation, a 20% withholding on capital transactions can be imposed. It *will be* imposed where failure to report three or more transactions occurs in a single year. Three or more failures are regarded as intentional negligence.

Let's go back to the example of our Treasury Bond sale above. Suppose a customer made three T-bond sales in a taxable year. One sale was $9,675 (a $235 loss); another was $9,885 (a $115 loss); and the third was $10,350 (a $350 gain). His cumulative loss and gain for the three sales would be exactly zero (-235-115+350). There would be no net tax consequence whatsoever. Realizing this, the investor decides not to report the three sales.

Three failures to report a capital transaction on one's Form 1040 will be noted by Big Brother's computer. Thereupon, the IRS can direct the broker to withhold 20% of the investor's gross proceeds. In the example case, the gross proceeds would be $30,000. Therefore, 20% of the $30,000 — which is $6,000 — would be withheld by the broker and paid over to the IRS. The amount withheld, however, is treated as prepayment credit against the investor's final taxes for the year. What does this do for government?

If there were no additional tax due — as could well be the case in the example presented — the entire $6,000 backup withholding would be refunded to the investor. It would take nine to 15 months after the withholding, before the refund would be paid. In the meantime, the government has held the investor's $6,000 *interest free*. At, say, 10% per annum ordinary interest, the government would derive $600 in unearned revenue. This is called the "withholding float" principle of TEFRA compliance.

Taxing Gross Proceeds

There is still another insidious purpose of broker reportings. The purpose is to tax the *gross proceeds* of those who underreport, or who do not report, or who do not report correctly. With Big Brother's computer, it is so easy to tax gross proceeds. *It is wrong* . . . but it is computer-easy, and difficult for a taxpayer to correct.

Most taxpayers are terrified of the IRS. They are easily intimidated by its computer printouts. The printouts are unintelligible, and are designed to shock taxpayers into prompt payment of additional tax, penalties, and interest without questioning the legitimacy of the computer demand.

To illustrate the effect, let's go back to the three T-bond sales above. The net gain and loss for tax purposes is zero. But, by not reporting the three sales, the computer will tax the $30,000 gross proceeds as though it were additional ordinary income. Suppose the taxpayer were in the 15% tax bracket (single), without the sales. With the sales, suppose the tax bracket jumped to 30% (single). Thus, the computer would demand $9,000 in *additional tax*. To this would be added the Section 6662 accuracy-related *penalty* of 20% (another $1,000). Since it would take from 18 to 24 months for the IRS to notify the taxpayer, there would be approximately $1,600 of *interest* to be paid. Altogether, a computer demand for $12,400.

You don't think this could happen?

It *did* happen!

It happened to an 86-year-old woman (widow), who was disabled and bedridden. When her daughter told her about the additional tax, she had a stroke. When she recovered, she told her daughter to draw down her life's savings and pay the computer demand.

Fortunately, the daughter went to a professional tax person to review the situation. The IRS was dead wrong. While the elderly woman did not report the T-bond sales on her Form 1040, she did report all of the interest income from the T-bonds. Some common sense could have been used by the IRS. Eventually, the matter was straightened out, and there was no additional tax to pay.

Broker Form 1099-B

How is a broker to report and withhold on the gross proceeds of a capital transaction? Answer: By a special tax form, of course.

The means for broker reporting is addressed by Regulation 1.6045-1(d)(2). Subheaded as **Transactional reporting**, it reads:

> *As to each sale with respect to which a broker is required to make a return of information under this section, the broker . . . shall show on Form 1099-B the name, address, and taxpayer identification of the customer for whom the sale was effected, the property sold, . . . the gross proceeds, sale date, and such other information as may be required on Form 1099-B, in the form, manner, and number of copies required by Form 1099-B.*

Form 1099-B carries the official heading: **Proceeds from Broker and Barter Exchange Transactions**. An edited version of the official form is presented in Figure 3.1.

PAYER'S name, address & zip code		YEAR		PROCEEDS FROM BROKER AND BARTER EXCHANGE TRANSACTIONS
		1a. Date of sale		
		1b. CUSIP No.		
PAYER'S Tax I.D. No.	RECIPIENT'S Soc. Sec. No.	2. Stocks, bonds, etc.		☐ Gross Proceeds ☐ Net Proceeds
RECIPIENT'S name, address & zip code		3. Bartering		4. Fed. tax withheld
		5. Description		
		Regulated Futures Contracts		
		6.	7.	8.	9.
Copy A	Copy B	Copy C	*Edited for instructional purposes*	

Fig. 3.1 - General Format/Content of Form 1099-B

Please study Figure 3.1 carefully. If you are an investor, and make any sales or exchanges or other transfers of a capital asset through a broker, *each transaction* will be reported to Big Brother on this form (or on subsequent amendments to it). Note that Box 1a requires the date of sale. Box 1b requires reporting the CUSIP Number (Committee on Uniform Security Identification Procedures). The ultimate IRS goal is to have all capital transactions in the U.S. be traceable through their gross proceeds and brokerage account numbers. Think about the totalitarian implications of this for awhile!

In Figure 3.1 particularly note Box 2: Stocks, bonds, etc. The "etc." means *all* capital transactions (commodities, currencies, collectibles) except barter exchanges (Box 3) and futures contracts (Boxes 6 through 9).

In the same space as Box 2, there are two check-boxes:

☐ *Gross proceeds*
☐ *Net proceeds*

The net proceeds are gross proceeds less broker commissions, closing costs, and option premiums. More frequently than not, these two check-boxes are left blank. If so, assume that gross proceeds are reported.

Box 5 requires a brief description of the transaction(s). The official instructions to Form 1099-B say:

If necessary, abbreviate the description so that it fits within Box 5.

At present, three copies of each Form 1099-B are required. Copy A goes to the Internal Revenue Service, Copy B goes to the recipient (investor/payee), and Copy C is retained by the preparing broker (payer) for his files. In practice, Copy B is the only physical piece of paper involved. "Copies" A and C are purely electronic media transmissions.

Computer Mismatching Problems

On an average slow stock-trading day in the U.S., some 100,000,000 (100 million) shares change hands on the New York and American exchanges. Another 20,000,000 (20 million) shares and equivalents change hands over the counter and through regional exchanges and market-to-market sales. Assuming an average of 100 shares per transaction, there could be as many as 300,000,000 (300 million) Form 1099-B's filed with the IRS each year (in 250 trading days). Can you not imagine the chaos and confusion that results?

Think of the inadvertent errors that are made. The broker himself/herself makes errors. The broker's computer makes errors.

The IRS key punch operators make errors. The overall result is a barrage of computer mismatching problems that boggles the mind.

The idea behind all of these 1099 forms is for the IRS's computer to cross-match the information on the 1099's with the information reported on each individual's tax return. This is the "compliance enforcement" aspect of the 1099's. If there is a mismatch, the computer automatically assesses an additional tax . . . plus penalty and interest.

The grand scheme is presented in Figure 3.2. It is the perfect dream for total government control over all U.S. investors.

Let us now exemplify the problem. Consider an investor who has made five capital transactions for the year (3 short-term and 2 long-term). His total proceeds from the five sales is $100,000. He made $15,000 profit on the three short sales; he suffered a $10,000 loss on the two long sales. For his own convenience, he groups the three short sales into one entry on Form 1040. He lists the average sales price of $25,000. He also groups the two long sales into one entry, and lists the average sales price of $5,000. His gain and loss entries are absolutely correct. He computes and pays the correct tax. What happens in the computer matching process? (Assume the taxpayer is in the 30% bracket.)

Some 18 to 24 months later, the IRS computer picks up the fact that five Form 1099-B's were submitted showing total proceeds of $100,000. It matches this information with the $30,000 total sales shown on the individual's Form 1040. It computes a reporting discrepancy of $70,000. The computer immediately asserts a deficiency demand for $21,000 in additional tax ($70,000 x 30%) plus, say, $3,000 in interest. No IRS human ever reads the proper gain and loss information on Form 1040. The computer does everything. When the taxpayer gets the Computer Demand, does he owe the additional tax and interest?

No. He does not.

He reported his proper gain and loss, and he paid the correct tax thereon. For his own convenience, he simply lumped his five transactions into two, and reported the average gross sales proceeds of each. What is so wrong with this? After all, the correct *taxable* amount was reported.

Which brings up the disturbing question. What is the real purpose of Form 1099-B? It does not — cannot — establish the correct tax. Nor does it verify actual reporting compliance.

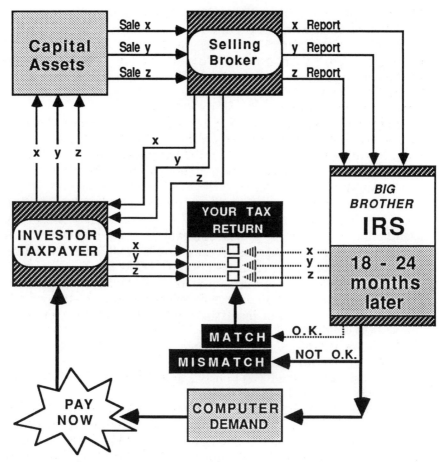

Fig. 3.2 - Scheme of IRS's "Computer Matching" of Sales Proceeds

The IRS Misperception

Glance again at Figure 3.1 showing the required entries on Form 1099-B. Then, from your own records, select a Form W-2 Wage and Tax Statement. Note the general similarity in format between your W-2 and the 1099-B.

A broker who pays the proceeds in a capital transaction is regarded by the IRS much the same as an employer who pays wages and other compensation for personal services. This is a basic failing in perception by the IRS. This misperception is the sole cause of a fundamental fault with Form 1099-B.

Capital transactions and wage income are tax treated much differently from each other. We particularly stressed this tax difference in Chapter I: Investor Defined. The IRS knows about this difference, but it looks the other way in its greed for computer power over taxpayers.

In capital transactions, tax applies only after netting of gains and losses, both short-term and long-term. In contrast, tax applies to wage income directly. Yet, in the IRS computer brain, the 1099-B gross proceeds are treated computationally exactly the same as W-2 gross wages.

To illustrate the incompatibility in tax treatment, let's go back to our five-transaction example above. For illustrative simplicity, assume that the taxpayer is in a constant 30% tax bracket. Recall that the broker-reported gross proceeds were $100,000. The broker properly submitted to the IRS five Form 1099-B's.

The correct taxable amount reported by the taxpayer on his Form 1040 was $5,000. This is the result of net-netting $15,000 of gain with $10,000 of loss. For the assumptions made, the correct tax on the $5,000 would be $1,500 (30% x $5,000).

If the $100,000 were all wages, as the IRS assumes, the computer tax would be $30,000.

Now do you see the basic injustice and fallibility of the computer compliance effort with Form 1099-B?

Turning the matter around, suppose the taxpayer matched exactly on his Form 1040 the gross proceeds reported on Forms 1099-B. In his preoccupation with exact matching, he erroneously reported the $15,000 capital gain as a $15,000 loss. The result would be an underpayment of tax by $900. (The per year capital loss limit is $3,000. So, 30% x $3,000 equals $900.)

Will the IRS computer pick up this erroneous underpayment?

No. It will not.

Our overall conclusion is that Form 1099-B serves no correct tax purpose whatsoever, where the taxpayer, broker, and IRS computer exactly match each other. Furthermore, the form openly invites *computer gamesmanship* by taxpayers who exact-match, but who intentionally underreport capital gains and overreport capital losses. This all goes back to the IRS misperception in the design and use of Form 1099-B.

Examine (Carefully) Your 1099-B

By and large, most taxpayers are reasonably conscientious in preparing and reporting information on their Form 1040's (with schedules attached). Now and then, for kicks, they may engage in some gamesmanship. But willful tax evasion and willful tax rebellion are not everyone's cup of tea. So, if one is an active investor, what does he do about the barrage of 1099-B's that he will receive?

Answer. He lives with the situation . . . and conforms to it. The IRS is paranoid about compliance enforcement through computer matching. It will not back down.

Other than amending the 1099-B's to include additional information, or to create other new 1099's and regulations, the IRS will not — and cannot — change its computer misperceptions. In our subsequent chapters, you will understand more fully why this is so. There are just too many accounting variables and special rules for determining capital gains and losses. There is no practical compliance alternative to the gross proceeds reporting.

Having to live with Form 1099-B does not mean that you have to live with the inevitable errors that will occur. You do not have to live with errors caused by brokers preparing the forms. Nor do you have to live with IRS errors in processing the forms.

You are supposed to receive from your broker a copy of each Form 1099-B that he prepares on you. The specific tax law on point is Section 6045(b): **Statements to be furnished to customers.** This section reads—

> *Every person making a return under . . . [broker reporting rules] . . . shall furnish to each customer whose name is required to be set forth in such return a written statement showing—*
> (1) *the name and address of the person required to make such return, and*
> (2) *the information required to be shown on such return with respect to such customer.*
> *The written statement . . . shall be furnished to the customer on or before January 31 of the year following the calendar year for which the return . . . was required to be made.*

When you receive each Form 1099-B, examine it carefully. Search diligently for "prime errors." These are errors in your Social Security number, errors in the gross proceeds paid, and errors in type of capital asset sold. If any such errors are found, insist that the broker correct the entry and *re-issue* a corrected Form 1099-B. To accomplish this, you may have to fight your way through the brokerage management and its computer system. If necessary, prepare a written complaint, and keep a copy in your records, should you need it for convincing the IRS of the broker's error.

An IRS problem is created when trying to correct broker errors. After some lapse of time, the broker sends in another Form 1099-B. He check-marks a headbox thereon as "CORRECTED." There is no provision on the corrected form to indicate (by cross reference) a prior (incorrect) Form 1099-B. What does the IRS do in this case?

It *adds* both the corrected and incorrect forms together! Then it looks for **both** of the broker forms being included on the taxpayer's return. Once the incorrect report is included, it can be "zeroed out."

Trying to correct the IRS on its computer foulups is a formidable task. There is no magic way of doing this. Eventually, two or three years later, you may have to deal with the IRS Problem Resolution Office.

Search for "Substitute Statements"

Brokerage firms are financial institutions. As such, they have a lot more clout with the IRS than individual taxpayers. Brokers have objected to the increased administrative cost imposed on them by the requirements of Form 1099-B (and other 1099's).

As a consequence of these objections, the IRS allows brokers to provide their clients with *equivalent substitute statements*. Generally, this equivalence is construed to mean a broker's regular confirmation statements. It is customary for brokers to provide confirmation statements of all transactions (buy, sell, exchange, etc.) executed for their clients. Hence, the IRS allows brokers to adapt their regular confirmation statements to the 1099-B reporting procedures.

Some brokerage firms computer-print the phrase "Form 1099" onto their regular year-end cumulative statements. Thereon is a preprinted footnote which reads:

When this statement is marked 1099, the information above will be filed with the Internal Revenue Service pursuant to federal law.

Other brokerage firms will prepare a consolidated year-end statement of all transactions for each client. In their own computer format, they will separate out the various 1099 reports. They will indicate specific dollar entries, blanks, or footnotes on sequential lines marked, such as:

	Amount	**Description**
• **Form 1099-A**	_____	_____
• **Form 1099-B**	_____	_____
• Form 1099-INT	_____	_____
• Form 1099-DIV	_____	_____
• Form 1099-OID	_____	_____
• Form 1099-MISC	_____	_____
• **Form 1099-S**	_____	_____

Thus, instead of issuing separate 1099 forms, one computer form with separated amounts is issued. This is an equivalent substitute statement for IRS reporting purposes.

There is no uniformity in format or placement of the reported information on these substitute statements. Each broker does that which is most compatible with his own internal computer programming and confirmation procedures. Many brokers "pump out" their confirmation statements on the slightest transactional pretense. Some do it monthly; some send duplicates; some send corrections; some send 5 to 10 computer sheets for every statement.

As an investor, you must search diligently through all substitute statements. You want particularly to separate out those marked "1099" in some manner. You must *read* all of the computer forms to do this. The IRS will not do it for you.

We cannot caution you too strongly to be on the alert for spotting that broker information which is submitted to the IRS. If you are not alert — and selective — the IRS will computer demand from you additional tax. The IRS computer will demand and demand until you reconcile the broker reports (right or wrong) with your own reportings.

Forms 1099-A and 1099-S

In the brokerage listing above, there are two other *transaction information* returns that we should tell you about. These are Forms 1099-A and 1099-S. Their official titles are:

1099-A: Acquisition or Abandonment of Secured Property
1099-S: Proceeds from Real Estate Transactions

These two information returns are arranged similarly to Form 1099-B, which we edited and abbreviated in Figure 3.1. However, the nomenclature on the "A" and "S" forms is different. Therefore, we depict these differences in Figure 3.3. Our purpose in Figure 3.3 is to make you aware that, as an investor, Forms 1099-A and 1099-S do exist. They will be used against you for computer-matching purposes, when applicable.

LENDER'S name, address & zip code	**YEAR** **FORM 1099-A**	ACQUISITION OR ABANDONMENT OF SECURED PROPERTY
	1. Date	2. Balance owing $
LENDER'S Tax I.D. No. · BORROWER'S Soc. Sec. No.	3. Gross foreclosure proceeds $	4. Appraisal value $
BORROWER'S name, address & zip code	5. Is borrower liable for repayment? ☐ yes ☐ no	
	6. Description of property	

FILER'S name, address & zip code	**YEAR** **FORM 1099-S**	PROCEEDS FROM REAL ESTATE TRANSACTIONS
	1. Date of closing	2. Gross proceeds $
FILER'S Tax I.D. No. · TRANSFEROR'S Soc. Sec. No.	3. Legal description of property	
TRANSFEROR'S name, address & zip code		
	4. Check if other property or services part of consideration ☐	

Fig. 3.3 - Key Entries on Forms 1099-A and 1099-S

Form 1099-A is for a transaction between a lender and a borrower, where the loan is secured by property of any kind. The secured property may be real estate, transport vehicles, productive machinery, electronic equipment, marketable securities, or other. The borrower (investor) pledges this property and uses the money to make other investments. If an "other investment" goes sour, the borrower either defaults on his repayment obligations or abandons his pledged property.

When a borrower defaults on his loan obligation or abandons his pledged property, the lender has the legal right to foreclose on, or to acquire, the property under the laws of the state where the property resides. These acquisitions of property through foreclosure or abandonment are treated as a sale by the investor, for capital accounting purposes. The borrower/investor has to tax report the transaction just like any other sale.

Whereas Form 1099-A is for foreclosures on and abandonments of property, Form 1099-S is for the intentional sales or exchanges of real estate. The real estate may be raw land, residential buildings, commercial buildings, industrial buildings, farm land, multi-unit residential structures, and other. Wherever and whenever legal title to real estate changes hands, the transaction is reported to the IRS on Form 1099-S. The report is made by the real estate broker, the title company, or an attorney who oversees the transaction and its "closing." Such reporting person or entity is called the *filer*.

If the investor (transferor) does not report on his own tax return the exact gross proceeds amount entered on the 1099-S, the IRS taxes the investor as though the reported figure were all capital gain. We know this is not right; you know it is not right; and the IRS knows it's not right. But that's what the Forms 1099-A, 1099-B, and 1099-S are all about. This is that "computer matching" enforcement dream of Figure 3.2.

Other Form 1099's (Income)

Also, previously, we listed four other Form 1099-type information returns. These were identified as 1099-INT, 1099-DIV, 1099-OID, and 1099-MISC. All of these are *income* reporting forms. They are not loss reporting forms, nor are they transaction (proceeds of sale) forms such as 1099-A, 1099-B, or 1099-S.

The official titles to the four income-reporting forms are—

1099-INT: Statement for Recipients of Interest Income

1099-DIV: Statement for Recipients of Dividends and Distributions

1099-OID: Statement for Recipients of Original Issue Discount

1099-MISC: Statement for Recipients of Miscellaneous Income

These income information returns are the kind that require annual reporting on an investor's tax return. Whether reported, not reported, or improperly reported, the forms are all subject to computer matching (Figure 3.2).

Unfortunately, investor problems are created with these income information returns. More often than not, they alter the capital accounting of the "cost or other" basis in one's investment(s). This creates cost confusion when the assets are sold or exchanged. Much depends on the types of investments and options exercised by the investor. For this reason, we will reserve discussion on these income/cost complications to the separate chapters which follow, on each class of investments.

Those Schedule K-1's

If you invest in conduit (pass-through) assets, a different system of information reporting to the IRS is used. This is the Schedule K-1 or "K-1" system of reporting. Instead of a broker or middleman doing the reporting (as in the 1099-series), the reports are prepared by each entity's tax manager. In the case of estates and trusts, the K-1's are prepared by the executor/trustee; limited partnerships by the general partner; and S corporations by the designated corporate officer.

For each type of conduit entity, there is a designated K-1 form. The official titles of these information returns are:

Sch. K-1 (Form 1041) — Beneficiary's Share of Income,
 [Estates and Trusts] Deductions, Credits, Etc.
Sch. K-1 (Form 1065) — Partner's Share of Income,
 [Limited Partnerships] Credits, Deductions, Etc.
Sch. K-1 (Form 1120S) — Shareholder's Share of Income,
 [S Corporations] Credits, Deductions, Etc.

As these official titles indicate, the K-1's report income, distributions (gains/losses from capital transactions), and deductions. These items are "pass through" matters assigned to each investor, in proportion to his capital share in the overall entity. Each K-1 form can accommodate up to 15 — yes, fifteen — separate items for computer matching. For most investors, the pass-through information is complicated, confusing, and misleading.

The K-1's expose the horrifying and ugly behavior of the IRS towards investors. Aside from containing information on portfolio income, operating income, and capital gains, the K-1's also report operating losses, certain deductions, business credits, and capital losses. All losses, deductions, and credits are tax beneficial to the participating investors. But guess what the IRS does with these K-1 benefits?

You probably already know the answer. The IRS ignores totally any of the K-1 entries which are beneficial to the investor. It selects *only* the income and gains for computer matching. It ignores and refuses to computer match the losses, deductions, and credits. How can one respect a government agency which abuses its computer-matching power the way the IRS does?

To make matters worse, the K-1's are not required to be completed and sent to investors — nor to the IRS — until April 15th each year. This contrasts with the 1099-series which are due by January 31st. The fact that most K-1's are issued just before the tax-filing deadline (April 15) means that much of the information is reported late by investors. This lateness aggravates the unholy mess of computer matching the K-1's with each investor's own return.

Nominee Reportings

It is bad enough having a broker or middleperson doing the transaction reportings to the IRS. Worse yet, there are situations where *you* — the reported-on person — have to report on other persons: your own family and friends. These situations are called *nominee* transactions.

A "nominee" is a person (investor/taxpayer) who is the designated recipient of the sales proceeds from a co-ownership transaction. If, for example, there are three co-owners who have pooled their money, one of the co-owners may take it upon himself/herself to be the nominee for the others. If no such voluntary designation is made, the reporting broker uses the name he knows, or selects the first name in alphabetical order. The "nominee" thereby becomes the person whose name and Social

Security number are reported to the IRS as receiving the entire sales proceeds.

To illustrate what we are getting at, let's take a very common example of nominee activities.

You are a reasonably astute investor held in much regard by your family, friends, and colleagues. Two of your friends get a hot investment tip. They approach you to pool their money with you to have you buy — through your broker — 500 shares of a new public offering of XYZ Biotech. Each of the three of you puts up $2,000. Sure enough, within 30 days, the XYZ stock triples in value. You instruct your broker to sell. After deducting his commission, he sends you a check for $17,628.

Whose name and Social Security number are going on the Form 1099-B (or any other 1099 form) when the broker reports the $17,628 sales proceeds to the IRS?

Answer: Your name, of course.

And who is going to pay tax on the $17,628?

You are . . . UNLESS.

Your alternative is to re-report one-third of the sale proceeds ($5,876) under the name and Social Security number of Friend A. You do likewise for Friend B. You do this as a **nominee filer**. That is, you prepare Form 1096: *Transmittal of U.S. Information Returns*, and attach to it a Form 1099-B for Friend A, and a Form 1099-B for Friend B (total of two attachments). You send the transmittal form with the two 1099's attached to the IRS. Mailing instructions on "Where to File" are on the back of Form 1096. You send each friend a copy of his 1099.

If you do not make the two re-reports as nominee, you wind up paying capital gains tax on $15,628 (17,628 - 2,000). By reporting on your friends to the IRS, you pay tax only on $3,876 (5,876 - 2,000).

You've got to admit it. The IRS has come up with a masterful scheme of tax farming.

4

SCHEDULE D (FORM 1040)

The Official Formatting Of Schedule D (Capital Gains And Losses) Is Dominated By 1099-B Transactions. Sufficient Lines Are Provided So That Each Separate Event Can Be Described And Reported In 7 Columnar Entries. Similarly For 1099-A And 1099-S Transactions. "Computer Matching" By The IRS Focuses On Your Column (d) Entries: Sales Price. This Makes Reconciliation Of Errors Essential. For Tax Results Best For Investors, Column (e) [Cost Or Other Basis] Is THE KEY ENTRY. Assets Held One Year Or Less Are Treated As "Short-Term"; All Others Are "Long-Term."

By far the most important single tax form for every investor is Schedule D (Form 1040). Its short title is Capital Gains and Losses. Its long title is: **Capital Gains and Losses and Reconciliation of Forms 1099-B**.

This long title alerts you to the importance of the IRS's computer in cross-checking the gross sale proceeds that each investor reports on his own return. We particularly stressed in the preceding chapter the importance of your computer matching those 1099-B forms.

There are three little headnotes below the long title which say:

▶ Attach to Form 1040
▶ See Instructions for Schedule D
▶ For more space . . ., get Schedule D-1

Every investor knows — or should know — what Form 1040 is. But in case you have not looked at it lately, it carries the heading: **U.S. Individual Income Tax Return**. There is a line in the Gross Income section on Page 1 of Form 1040 which reads:

Capital gain or (loss); attach Schedule D

Since this is not a forms-filling-out book, we are not going to tell you how to fill out Schedule D (1040) for your own particular set of transactions. But we are going to tell you some things about the form which you will not find in the official instructions. We want you to understand the form so that you can use it to *your* best tax advantage. If you use Schedule D properly, you can spare yourself a lot of computer harassment by the IRS.

Introduction to Schedule D

In a nutshell, Schedule D (Form 1040) constitutes a summary of all capital transactions that occurred during the taxable year. Only sales, exchanges, and other dispositions are reported on Schedule D. Acquisitions are not included — not even mentioned — until the year of disposition. This means that one can acquire assets at will without reporting them (unless they produce income, and then only the income is reported). In the end, one can select the year of sale that does him the most tax good.

Officially, Schedule D (1992) consists of seven parts, namely:

Part I   — Short-term Gains and Losses
Part II   — Long-term Gains and Losses
Part III — Summary of Parts I and II
Part IV — Computation: Maximum Capital Gains Rate
Part V   — Computation of Capital Loss Carryovers
Part VI — Election Out of Installment Method
Part VII — Reconciliation of Barter Transactions

Parts I and II are on Page 1, whereas Parts III, IV, V, VI,and VII are on Page 2. Thus, there are *two* full pages to Schedule D: front and back. While this may seem like a trivial comment, there is a reason for our pointing this out to you.

Computers today routinely print on only one side of the paper. The IRS computer prints on one side; your broker's computer prints on one side; and your own computer prints on one side. Because of this one-side-only computer printing, persons using/processing Schedule D often fail to turn the form over (to page 2). Believe it or not, IRS processors themselves often fail to turn to Page 2 . . . of their own official forms! This results in erroneous computer printouts being mailed to you by the IRS . We are calling your attention to this little quirk now, so that you will not fail to turn Schedule D over to its Page 2. It contains many "for-the-record" computations. We will not be discussing Page 2 (Parts III through VI) in this chapter.

Actually, Parts I and II on Page 1 are not all there is to Schedule D. There is a **Continuation Sheet for Schedule D,** called "Schedule D-1." Part I of Schedule D-1 takes up all of its Page 1; Part II takes up all of Page 2 of Schedule D-1. Thus, there is a continuation form to Schedule D which itself has two pages: front (for short-term) and back (for long-term).

Parts I and II on Schedules D and D-1 have approximately the same total number of transaction entry lines. Part I — for short-term transactions — has about 60 lines; Part II — for long-term transactions — also has about 60 lines. Altogether, Schedule D is designed to accommodate up to 120 Form 1099-B capital transactions in a given taxable year. If this is not enough, you can add additional Schedule D-1's and mark them sequentially as D-1 (#1), D-1 (#2), D-1 (#3), and so on.

The unwritten message on the official Schedule D is very clear. **Every single capital transaction must be separately entered and described.** If, for example, your broker lists 10 transactions together on a substitute 1099-B and gives you a single summary, you have to enter each transaction separately on Schedule D and D-1. This is the way the IRS computer is going to see the transaction: one entry blip at a time. The IRS never sees the Form 1099-B (or its substitute) that your broker sends to you. The IRS sees only electronic filing blips on magnetic media.

Total All 1099 Amounts

In Figure 4.1, we present a bird's-eye view of Schedule D, Page 1. We show Parts I and II in outline form only. We also show a headnote caution for all Forms 1099-B (and 1099-S).

In each part (I and II), we show a subtotal line for the disposition proceeds (sales price) from all separately entered 1099-B (or 1099-S) transactions. We indicate the subtotal lines with the letter "X" for Part I, and the letter "Y" for Part II. (On the official

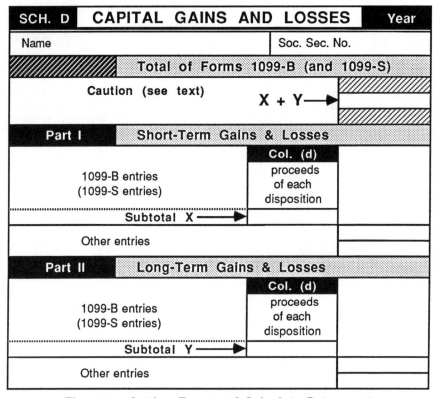

Fig. 4.1 - Outline Format of Schedule D (page 1)

Schedule D's, the subtotals appear on designated line numbers (which change from year to year.)

What we really want you to focus on in Figure 4.1 is the headnote: **Caution.** This caution on the official form reads—

Add the following amounts reported to you for ___(year)___ o n Forms 1099-B and 1099-S (or on substitute statements):
(a) proceeds from transactions involving stocks, bonds, and other securities, and
(b) gross proceeds from real estate transactions not reported on another form or schedule.
If this total does not equal the total of lines [X] and [Y], Column (d), attach a statement explaining the difference.

Our first suggestion is: Don't attach any statement for reconciliation purposes, even if you think you need one. To attach such a statement that the IRS computer can read, you'd have to essentially duplicate the entry spaces (line and column) on the official form. It is much simpler to use a separate entry line on Schedule D or D-1 to show each reconciliation that you need to show. We'll give specific examples below.

The official caution for computer-matching reconciliation derives from Column (d) of Schedule D or D-1. This column is officially titled: *Sales price (see instructions)*. The instructions tell you to use either the gross sales price or the net sales price (gross less commissions and premiums), whichever your broker reports to you on each Form 1099-B, Form 1099-S, or its substitute. The instructions also tell you—

Be sure to add all sales price entries . . . [in] *column (d), . . .* [and] *enter the totals on lines* [X] *and* [Y].

The whole idea behind these official instructions is that you have to do the reconciliation yourself. You add up, one by one, all of your entries in Column (d): Sales price. Then you check and cross-check to see that your total exactly matches the total which your broker(s) reported to the IRS. It is an absolute waste of time to try to get your broker(s) to help you in this regard. Take what the broker's computer gives you, right or wrong, and you "force fit" as necessary. Your goal is to stop cold any computer harassment from the IRS, should your Column (d) totals not match the grand totals that your broker(s) reported.

Direct-Entry Columns

In Figure 4.2, we present the columnar entries that appear in Parts I and II of Schedules D and D-1. Do note that there are seven such columns. Each column on the official form is alphabetically labeled exactly as we show in Figure 4.2. Please take a moment to actually read these columnar headings. They are self-explanatory. We'll be making frequent reference to them (re Forms 1099-B).

We have designated the arrangement in Figure 4.2 as "direct-entry" transactions. This means that for each 1099-B transaction, at least six of the seven columns must be filled. Obviously, for the same transaction, you cannot have both a gain and a loss. You have one or the other: *either* Column (f) for loss or Column (g) for gain.

Sch. D (1040)	CAPITAL GAINS & LOSSES					
Part I **Part II**	Direct-entry Transactions (1099-B)					
(a)	(b)	(c)	(d)	(e)	(f)	(g)
Description	Date Bought	Date Sold	Sales Price	Cost or Other Basis	LOSS	GAIN

Amounts from Sch. D-1 ➤

Total amount in (f) and in (g) < >

Subtract (f) from (g); enter net ➤

Total of Col. (d) ➤

Fig. 4.2 - Columnar Entries for 1099-B Transactions

There may be occasions where you have neither a gain nor a loss. A good example is pure return of capital or reversing a 1099-B error. In such case(s), you enter "zero" in *both* the gain and loss columns. Where there is a zero in Columns (f) and (g), the IRS computer skips over that horizontal line entry. Otherwise, if both are left blank, the IRS computer will use the Column (d) entry sales price and attribute it to Column (g) gain, and tax you accordingly.

For instructional clarity, we have rearranged and slightly edited the lower portion of Figure 4.2 relative to the official form. However, the technical and arithmetic substance is correct. We want you to see more clearly that there are four functional aspects of the direct-entry columns on Schedule D. The first of these aspects, of course, is that each 1099-B transaction is a separate 6-column horizontal-line entry of its own.

The second functional aspect of the Figure 4.2 arrangement relates to Schedule D-1. The bottom-line amounts from all Schedules D-1 (if more than one) are entered on the very last horizontal line of columnar entries on Schedule D. Part I from D-1 goes to Part I on Schedule D; Part II from D-1 goes to Part II. So, don't forget to bring your Schedule D-1 amounts forward to Schedule D. This is a common oversight by multiple-transaction investors. The IRS computer will not bring the D-1 information forward for you, and so will tax you twice.

The third functional aspect of Figure 4.2 is the gain and loss netting. In each of Parts I and II, the loss Column (f) is subtotaled, and the gain Column (g) is subtotaled. At the subtotal line, there may be an entry in each of the gain/loss columns. If so, the two columns are netted to give either a net gain or a net loss. There is a net gain or loss for Part I, and a separate net gain or loss for Part II. This netting and offsetting — dollar for dollar — of gains and losses can be a major tax advantage for astute investors.

The fourth aspect of Figure 4.2 is the special line box for totaling *all* Column (d) entries. There is a subtotal line box for Part I, and a separate subtotal box for Part II on the official Schedule D. The two Column (d) subtotal boxes are THE FOCUS TARGETS for computer matching by the IRS. (At this point, we urge that you glance back at Figure 3.2.) Do not leave these Column (d) subtotal boxes blank unless one or the other (Part I or Part II) is truly inapplicable.

If you've made any 1099-B transactions during the taxable year, and you leave both of the Column (d) subtotal boxes blank, you surely know by now what will happen. You will get a computer demand for additional tax based on the entire grand total proceeds broker reported. You may get an explanatory statement to the effect that: "The IRS cannot identify your capital transaction(s) and reconciliation(s) on Schedule D." Then it is up to you to either pay the additional tax or correct your Schedule D by filling in the applicable Column (d) subtotals.

Example Reconciliations

Most investors dread the 1099-B computer demands from the IRS. It is not that they want to avoid paying their correct tax; it is just that most of the 1099-B computer-matching demands are in error. Trying to correct these errors through the IRS or the brokerage firm(s) is a hopeless and frustrating task. Our suggestion is: Don't even try. You are better off correcting the errors that you can, on your own. The following examples are some of the reconciliation actions you can take, without consulting anyone.

Example 1. Often a brokerage firm will cash in a bond (or other debt instrument) for you at its face value. If you paid face value at the time you bought it, and you get face value back, you have neither gain nor loss. It is "return of capital." Yet, the broker reports the face value to the IRS as the sales price. Suppose the amount is $10,000. To satisfy the IRS computer, you show in Column (d) the amount of $10,000. You also show in Column (e) the amount of $10,000. Then enter "zero" in each of Columns (f) and (g). In Column (a) description, enter: *Return of capital.*

Example 2. You instructed your broker to sell some stock for which you paid $3,000. He makes the sale and sends you a check for $3,469 (net after his commission). Thus, your true gain was $469. When the 1099-B is prepared, the brokerage firm reports the sale amount to the IRS as $4,369. This is an obvious $900 transpositional error (4,369 - 3,469) . . . in your disfavor. You add this $900 error to your $3,000 investment amount by entering $3,900 into Column (e). You show the broker reported amount of $4,369 in Column (d). Your gain in Column (g) is $469 (4,369 - 3,900), which is correct. In Column (a) description, enter: *Sales price error <900>.*

Example 3. Your broker makes an acknowledged key punch error. For your transaction, he punched in $10,000 instead of $1,000. After receiving your confirmation statement, you call the broker and he computer corrects the transaction to $1,000. In the meantime, the central clearing office reports $11,000 of 1099-B transactions to the IRS. You paid $2,500 for the product, which means you have a loss of $1,500. On your Schedule D, you report $11,000 in Column (d) and $12,500 (11,000 + 1,500) in Column (e). Your loss in Column (f) is $1,500 (12,500 - 11,000). In Column (a) description, enter: *1099-B error <10,000>.*

Example 4. At the end of the year, the mutual fund that you're in sent you a 1099-B showing a total of $98,362 in sale/redemption/rollover proceeds. From your records, which you diligently kept, you can only identify $90,300. There is a "missing transaction" of $8,062 (98,362 - 90,300) somewhere. Your records show that you indeed net gained $6,500 "plus" on all of the transactions. In this case, you make two separate entries in Column (d): $90,300 and $8,062. In Column (e), corresponding to $90,300, you enter $83,800 for a Column (g) gain of $6,500

(90,300 - 83,800). In Column (e), corresponding to $8,062, you enter a fictitious amount such as $8,000. This will produce a small fictitious gain of $62. (This is the loose change "plus" on the true $6,500 gain.) Correspondingly, in Column (a) description, enter: *Unable to identify.*

Example 5. You loan a trustworthy investor friend $2,000. He buys stock in his employer company which issues him the certificates direct. When the stock reaches about $3,500 your friend turns the stock certificates over to you. He tells you to sell them, take your money, and return the difference. You turn the certificates over to your broker, who sends you a check for $3,689 (net of commission). You take your $2,000 and return $1,689 to your friend. The broker reports a 1099-B sale of $3,689 in your name and social security number. You enter in Column (d) the $3,689 and also enter it in Column (e). Put zeros in each of Columns (f) and (g). In Column (a) description, enter: *Nominee sale.*

None of the five examples above are hypothetical. They occur every day in the frenzied world of 1099-B computer matching. For recapitulation purposes, we present all five of our examples in Figure 4.3. The whole idea is to "force fit" your Column (d) entries to whatever is 1099-B reported, right or wrong. The Figure 4.3-type entries constitute "adequate disclosure" should, several years later, the IRS uncover the errors that it or your broker(s) made.

Importance of Column (e)

For computer-matching purposes, Column (d) — sales price — is the important entry. But for gain-loss arithmetic purposes, Column (e) — cost or other basis — is THE important entry on your Schedule D . . . and on Schedule D-1 (if applicable). This one column alone can dominate your tax consequences. From this column, the netting of all capital gains and capital losses accrues.

You should sense right away that if there is no entry — or a low entry — in Column (e), your net gain will be higher than proper. Your net loss will be lower than proper. Columns (f) LOSS and (g) GAIN are obtained directly from the difference between Columns (d) and (e).

If you will look on the official tax form itself, you will see that Column (e) is headed:

	1099-B ENTRIES ON SCHEDULE D						
	Columnar headings as they appear in Fig. 4.2						
	(a)	(b)	(c)	(d)	(e)	(f)	(g)
1	Return of capital	*	*	10,000	10,000	- 0 -	- 0 -
2	Sales price error <900>			4,369	3,900		469
3	1099-B error <10,000>			11,000	12,500	1,500	
4	XYZ fund			96,360	83,800		6,500
4'	Unable to identify			8,062	8,000		62
5	Nominee Sale			3,689	3,689	- 0 -	- 0 -
	Col. (d) Total ⟶						

* Enter specific date(s), as applicable. Otherwise, enter N/A (not applicable), Var (various), or U/K (unknown) , as appropriate.

Fig. 4.3 - Example Reconciliation Entries on Schedule D

Cost or other basis (see instructions)

The official instructions thereto read, in part:

In general, the cost or other basis is the cost of the property plus purchase commissions, improvements, and minus depreciation, amortization, and depletion. . . . If you do not use cash cost, please attach an explanation of your basis. . . . For more information, get Publication 551, **Basis of Assets.**

IRS Publication 551 is one government document which is quite well prepared on a complex subject. Every investor/taxpayer who uses Schedule D should have a copy of it in his/her files. It is an excellent summary of all important basis accounting rules.

From a tax jargon point of view, the term "basis" is more frequently used than cost. This is because cost is usually associated with the initial acquisition of property, whereas basis includes cost plus "adjustments" after acquisition . . . up to the time of sale.

One's "basis," therefore, is his accounting reference for establishing gain or loss upon disposition of investment property.

The importance of Column (e) is why we devoted an entire chapter (Chapter 2: Cost When Sold) to presenting the fundamentals on this one entry alone. While the IRS computer can match your Column (d) entries, it **cannot** match your Column (e) entries. Until such time as the IRS takes it upon itself to demand a report on every acquisition of an investment asset, and a report on every adjustment thereto during its period of holding, there is no way in the world that the IRS can computer match your Column (e). Therefore, you are entirely on your own on this matter.

1099-A and 1099-S Entries

Although the formatting of Schedule D is dominated by 1099-B transactions, there are also computer-matching requirements for 1099-A and 1099-S transactions. True, these latter transactions are fewer in number, but they (usually) are greater in sales price magnitude than the 1099-B's.

As you may recall from the previous chapter, the 1099-A and 1099-S transactions are—

1099-A: Acquisition or Abandonment of Secured Property
1099-S: Proceeds from Real Estate Transactions

For computer-matching reasons, for each and every 1099-A or 1099-S form issued, there needs to be a separate line of columnar entries, exactly as depicted in Figure 4.2. Your Column (d) entry (sales price) is the target for IRS matching.

In Parts I and II on Schedule D, there are bold-printed items which read:

Other Transactions [such as Form 1099-A, Form 6781, etc.] *Include* [with Form 1099-B] *Real Estate Transactions* [from] *Form 1099-S.*

The general instructions thereto say—

[1099-A] *If you received a Form 1099-A from your lender, you may have a gain or loss to report because of the acquisition* [by foreclosure] *or abandonment.*
[1099-S] *Enter sales and exchanges of . . . real estate transactions reported to you on Form(s) 1099-S or on an equivalent statement, unless you reported them on . . .* [other forms].

As in the case of all information-reporting forms, there are error probabilities by the person or entity doing the reporting. The 1099-A's and 1099-S's are no exception.

The error likelihood on Form 1099-A has to do with confusion over the applicable Column (d) "sales price." The form has *three* separate boxes for entering dollar amounts. These boxes are form-labeled as:

☐ Balance of principal owing, $
☐ Gross foreclosure proceeds, $
☐ Appraisal value, $

If the lender completes only one of the $-sign boxes, there is no Column (d) entry problem for you. But if the lender completes two or more of the $-boxes, for whatever reason, each dollar amount should be separately entered on Column (d). Then, it is up to you to reconcile as appropriate, along the lines of Figure 4.3.

Co-Owner Errors: 1099-S

The error likelihood on Form(s) 1099-S is much greater, and the effect more devastating, than on either 1099-A or 1099-B. This is because a 1099-S shows *gross proceeds* from the sale or exchange of real estate. In such transactions, the dollar amounts reported to the IRS can range from $100,000 to $1,000,000 . . . or more. The computer demands for tax on these amounts can be horrifying.

Certain 1099-S errors arise partly from the fact that there are multiple-type filers of the form. A 1099-S filer may be an agent, a broker, a title company, an attorney, or — in the case of direct seller/buyer transactions — the county official accepting new title to the property for public recordation. Any of these filers could misconstrue the entries intended in the boxes for (a) gross proceeds,

(b) legal description, and (c) other property and services received (by the transferor).

More typically, however, 1099-S errors result from reporting gross proceeds in those transactions involving two or more co-owners. (A husband and wife married at time of a 1099-S transaction are tax treated as one owner.)

When there is more than one owner, invariably there is some foul-up in the correct ownership interest of each, at time of disposition. There is also a mixup in social security numbers. If there are two or more co-owners, whose name and social security number goes on the 1099-S form?

To be correct for tax purposes, the filer should report each co-owner's prorata share of the gross proceeds on a *separate* 1099-S. If there is cooperation and understanding of the prorata tax consequences among the co-owners, a separate 1099-S for each would work out well.

But, if there is any disharmony between the co-owners — as there often is when a large amount of money is involved — the filer is cornered into a dilemma. He then has no choice but to report the total gross proceeds under the name and social security number of that co-owner first named on the title instrument of the property conveyed. When this happens, a *nominee sale* results to that portion which is not owned by the reported-on owner.

For example, suppose there are three co-owners: A, B, and C. Their respective "tentative" ownership interests are 50%, 30%, and 20%. The 1099-S reporting is a $300,000 sale. There is dickering among the co-owners as to their exact prorata share of selling expenses and net proceeds. Exasperated by all of this, the filer reports the $300,000 total proceeds under the social security number of Owner A.

What does Owner A do?

Answer: On Owner A's Schedule D, he enters the $300,000 figure in Column (d). Then in Column (e) [Cost or other basis], he reports his own tax basis **plus** $150,000 for nominee sales [30% + 20% of the $300,000]. Thereupon, Owner A himself becomes a 1099-S filer. He prepares two separate 1099-S forms: one to Owner B and one to Owner C. On Owner B's form, Owner A reports $90,000 (30% x $300,000) as gross proceeds. On Owner C's form, Owner A reports $60,000 (20% x $300,000) as gross proceeds. It is then up to Owners B and C to do their own 1099-S reporting on their own Schedule D's.

Other Related Forms

On each of Parts I and II of Schedule D, there are designated lines for entering gain and loss amounts from other forms. The designations are single-column entries: either Column (f) LOSS or Column (g) GAIN. There are no corresponding Column (d) or Column (e) entries whatsoever. The reason for this absence is that the related forms contain other than capital gain/loss information on them. The use of related forms is in keeping with the summary character of Schedule D, mentioned in the beginning of this chapter.

We present in Figure 4.4 a listing of those related forms that dovetail onto Schedule D. Needless to say, we cannot discuss these forms at this time. There are too many of them, and they are too diverse. We will discuss most — if not all — in later chapters. Figure 4.4 is intended to be instructive only as an introduction at this point.

Do note in Figure 4.4 that several of the entry spaces in the loss column are cross-hatched. This means that loss entries are not applicable. For example, the first form listed (1099-DIV) has a reporting box for capital *gain* distributions. These are dividend-type distributions made by regulated investment companies such as mutual funds. Only capital gains can be passed through to individual investors: not capital losses.

In contrast, the next-to-last listing in Figure 4.4 is for capital losses only: no gains. The entry intended is the amount of capital loss carryover, if any, from an investor's prior year Schedule D. The loss computations derive from Part V (of Schedule D), and; may be short-term or long-term, or both. Carryforward capital losses occur when the netting of gains and losses results in a net-net loss in excess of $3,000 for a given year. More on this subject in Chapter 11: Treatment of Losses.

Be aware that some of the indicated forms in Figure 4.4 apply to one transaction at a time. Take, for example, an investor who has four limited partnerships. Partnerships report their capital transactions on Schedule K-1 (Form 1065). A copy of each Schedule K-1 is sent to the IRS. Thus, our investor would have to summarize four K-1's and report the net capital gain or net capital loss on Schedule D. The presumption is that the investor will organize and key his K-1's so that the amount report on Schedule D can be backed up (when called upon for substantiation).

Figure 4.4 raises an interesting computer-matching question. "What about those broker reports?" Since there are no Column (d)

Sch. D (1040)	CAPITAL GAINS & LOSSES			
Page 1	**Gains and Losses From Related Forms**			
Form(s) Attached	**No.**	**Description**	**(f) LOSS**	**(g) GAIN**
1099 - DIV		Capital gain distributions	//////	
2119		Gain from personal residence	//////	
4684		Gain from casualties and thefts	//////	
4797		Gain from business property	//////	
6252		Gain from installment sales	//////	
6781		Futures contracts and straddles		
8824		Gain / loss : Like-kind exchanges		
K-1 (1041)		Gain / loss : Estates & trusts		
K-1 (1065)		Gain / loss : Partnerships		
K-1 (1120 S)		Gain / loss : Small corporations		//////
Pt.IV, Sch.D		Loss carryover : prior year(s)		
Other				
//////		Total amount in (f) and in (g) ⟶ < >		
Total No. of forms involved		**Subtract (f) from (g); enter net ⟶**		
				//////

Fig. 4.4 - Other Forms That Dovetail Onto Schedule D

entries, how are the broker reportings reconciled with what the investor reports on his related forms?

Answer: We are going to let you think about this for awhile.

Holding Periods I and II

Throughout this chapter, we have made reference to Parts I and II of Schedule D. Part I, recall, is officially designated as *short-term* gains and losses; Part II as *long-term* gains and losses. The short-term, long-term aspects constitute holding period classifications.

The concept of holding periods raises two practical questions. One: What is the distinction between short-term and long-term? Two: Why is the distinction important?

As to the first question, the distinctive time frame is one year. Assets held one year or less are regarded as short-term holdings. Those held more than one year are long-term holdings.

The period of holding an asset starts on the **day after** the date of legal acquisition. Legal title may be in the form of physical possession, a right to possession, a trade date, a book entry date, a recording date, or some other specific traceable date when title passed from offerer to acquirer. The holding period ends when the reverse is true. The **day of disposition** counts as part of the holding period.

As to the second question (Why important?), there are three reasons. The first reason is that inflation indexing is never allowed for short-term holdings.

The second reason is that a number of "associated" forms which dovetail onto Schedule D (as in Figure 4.4), direct the tax computations in such a way that gives a slight advantage to long-term holdings over short term. A good example is Form 6781: Gains and Losses From Section 1256 Contracts and Straddles. The Form 6781 computations direct that 40% of the net gain or loss be treated as short term, and that 60% be treated as long term.

The third reason why the length of holding is important is that there are always tax incentives afoot to encourage longer holding periods. The purpose is to reduce volatility in the financial markets. For example, in early 1990, a Senate proposal was introduced to reinstate Section 1202 of the tax code. The reinstated section would be titled: Reduction in Capital Gains Tax for Noncorporate Taxpayers. The proposal step-reduced the amount of taxable gain for 1-year holdings, 2-year holdings, and 3-year holdings. Consequently, there seems to be general consensus that long-term holdings should receive at least some preferential treatment over short-term holdings. On this issue, however, the "tax dust" never seems to settle.

As of 1992, the maximum tax rate on net long-term capital gain is 28%. This compares with the maximum rate of 31% on net short-term gain. When 6-digit or more gross proceeds are involved, this 3% long-term-rate preferential treatment can be significant.

5

ALLOCATION DISCIPLINE

> **Stringent "Cost Allocation" Is Required Where Multiple Assets Evolve From A Single Asset Or From The Bulk Acquisition Of Different Assets. This Presents An Accounting Challenge Where "Modifications" Are Made Before Sale . . . When The Sale Dates Differ. Investor Self-Discipline With Good Records Is Needed. Depending On The Facts And Circumstances Of Each Acquisition/Disposition, Special Allocation Rules Apply. If "You" Do Not Do The Allocation Yourself, The IRS Will Horrify You With Its Nonallocation.**

In the preceding chapter, at least two messages should have come through. One is that every disposition of an investment asset constitutes a separate tax accounting event of its own. All cost data on that event must be separate and apart from all other events: be they similar or dissimilar in time and character. That's why there are so many 7-columnar entry lines on Schedule D (1040).

The second message (founded on Chapter 2) is that Column (e) — cost or other basis — is the most important entry item for an investor. Getting the Column (e) information correct is paramount to deriving the best capital-gain/capital-loss benefits. But Column (e) is where certain *allocation* problems arise.

Most investors acquire their investments in class groupings. That is, they become emotionally attached to a particular class of assets — gold coins, rare art, raw land, antiques, collectibles — based on hunches of "hidden values" that will spring forth in the future. With great expectations, they don't buy just one item and hold on to it. They spread their risks by buying several items of a given class, irregularly and intermittently over time. And they sell irregularly as the opportunity arises. In the meantime their costs and expenses become commingled and confused. They are unable to allocate their capitalized costs separately to each item sold.

In this chapter, therefore, we want to focus on the problems of allocating cost at time of sale. To help simplify the explanations, we will dwell on sterile assets only. Sterile assets are those which generate no income, or virtually no income, while being held. As we'll see in subsequent chapters, the generation of income during holding aggravates the cost allocation problems. The longer the holding period, the greater the amount of discipline needed for allocating commingled costs upon disposition.

Introductory Illustration

The nature of sterile investments is such that you may acquire them in one form but, when disposed of, they are a conglomerate of multiple forms. Or, vice versa. Between acquisition and disposition there may be an evolution of changes, discoveries, and interests which clouds your true investment in each asset sold. When this happens, allocation for tax accounting becomes severe. The tendency is to think only of initial cost.

Let us illustrate the problem of "cost commingling" with a plausible example. We will use $10,000 as your initial investment. The amount could be $100, $1,000, or $100,000. The allocation principles would be the same.

Suppose you bought a rare landscape painting, a true original, that cost $10,000. You bought it through a reputable art dealer who provided you with a bill of sale and certification of authenticity. The artist who created it is long deceased. It cannot be recreated again. You buy it strictly as an investment, expecting it to go up in value with time. Meanwhile, you hang it on the wall in your residence to show to friends and guests.

One of your friends sees it who is a commercial photographer. He wants to take color photos of it and sell them as part of his ongoing business. He offers to buy exclusive rights to photograph your painting. You think about the offer. You decide to sell the photo rights for $2,000. You now have the emergence of an allocation problem for tax purposes. You have to allocate the cost of $10,000 between the painting itself and the rights to photograph it.

Suppose a referral of one of your friends is in the fine arts printing business. He sees the painting on your wall. He wants to buy the rights to reprint it in actual size and sell the reprints with different framing from yours. After much hesitation, you agree. He pays you $3,000. Now you have *three* capital assets: the painting, photo rights, and reprint rights. The allocation of your $10,000 takes on added complexity.

A year or two later, one of your close and trusted friends, seeing the appreciation potential in your painting, wants to buy an ownership share in it. He offers you $5,000 on the spot for a fractional share. He wants a 50% share, but you counter with 30%. Now you have complicated the allocation of your initial $10,000 one step further.

The Complications Go On

Because of the increasing interest in your landscape painting, you decide to have a special tripod stand made for it with self-contained accent lighting fixtures thereon. You design the stand yourself, then have a specialty shop fabricate it for you. When complete, you can move the painting around from room to room, or lend it to friends for their house guests to observe and enjoy. You pay $5,000 for the stand out of your receipts above. You have now created still another capital asset: the self-contained display stand.

While on display in the home of one of your friends, an entrepreneur in the specialty furniture business sees your stand and likes it. He likes the painting but he likes the stand much more. So much in fact that he offers to buy your design and mass produce it for sale. He offers you $10,000 and provides you with a guaranteed cashier's check. You ponder this quite awhile before accepting.

After a few more months on display in your friend's home, word comes to you that an "unidentified buyer" loves your painting and stand so much that he is willing to pay $60,000 for it. He offers green paper cash: 600 one-hundred-dollar bills. Would you refuse such an offer? After all, you never intended to keep the painting and stand forever. You have had it more than five years, so, "Why not sell it?" you say to yourself.

Somehow, prudence gets the upper hand over greed. You decide to consult with your tax man or other counselor/advisor whose opinion you respect. He warns you about the unidentified buyer. Such person might be a foreign oil sheik; he might be a broker for organized crime; he might be a drug trafficker trying to launder "hot money." He might also be an undercover agent for the Internal Revenue Service. Accordingly, you are advised to accept only a cashier's check for the $60,000 and provide the buyer with a bill of sale, giving full particulars. This is agreeable with the buyer.

You are intoxicated with the success of your investment. You put up $10,000 and got back a total of $80,000 (the $60,000 plus the 2-, 3-, 5-, and 10-thousand dollar deals).

You acquired one asset initially, but you disposed of *six* assets. Each of the six assets was entirely different from your original asset. You disposed of—

1. A 70% ownership interest in the painting,
2. Exclusive rights to photograph it,
3. Actual-size reproduction/reprint rights,
4. A 100% ownership in the display stand,
5. Design drawings to the stand, and
6. Reproduction rights to the stand.

How do you allocate the $10,000 and the $80,000 for tax purposes? The answer(s) will be found in bits and pieces in the paragraphs below.

Why Self-Discipline Needed

A cavalier taxpayer takes the position that it is up to the IRS to worry about allocation details. The truth is, the IRS does not worry about any matter that is in your best tax interest. The IRS's position is this: "Either you make the allocation of cost, ownership, time, and so on, on an acceptable basis, or we will allocate in a manner that will derive maximum tax revenue."

So, you have a choice. Either you do the allocation yourself, or the government will *not* do it for you. In the illustration above, the government could tax you on as much as $80,000 . . . in ordinary income. You could be deprived of all capital gain benefits.

If you report the painting/stand sale on Schedule D as one lump sum, you would be taxed on a capital gain of $70,000. If you set your mind to it, and allocate properly, you could report as many as six sales in as many tax years. You could take advantage of separate capital gain/loss netting each year, plus making adjustments for additional costs as you incur them, plus indexing if (particularly) the initial asset was held more than five years. At the end of the chain of sales, it is conceivable that you could be taxed on as little as $30,000 in net capital gain.

Actually, there is no direct statutory authority for the IRS to allocate capital assets to maximize tax revenue. The "authority" to do so derives from case law. Tax Courts invariably hold that if a taxpayer does not allocate on his own, he is not in a position to complain about how the IRS might allocate for him.

The nearest statutory authority for this position by IRS is Section 6020(b)(1): **Authority of Secretary to execute returns**. Except for substituting "IRS" for "Secretary," this section reads in full as—

If any person fails to make any return required by an internal revenue law or regulation made thereunder at the time prescribed therefor, or makes, willfully or otherwise, a false or fraudulent return, the [IRS] *shall make such return from* [its] *own knowledge and from such information as* [it] *can obtain through testimony or otherwise. Any return so made and subscribed by the* [IRS] *shall be prima facie good and sufficient for all legal purposes.*

There is always danger in letting a government agency like the IRS perform any tax accounting task that you should do yourself. It will never be fair and impartial. It will be *always biased* for maximum revenue. When the IRS does it, it "shall be prima facie" good and sufficient. You know this is not true.

The official position is that a taxpayer may be trying to avoid or evade taxes if he fails to make proper allocation among his various capital assets. If this is so — or is perceived to be so — an "accuracy penalty" can be added to the maximum tax computed by the IRS.

It behooves every investor/taxpayer, therefore, to take the time and exercise the self-discipline of proper allocation. There is a multitude of special rules for doing so; we can only cover those which are basic and more common.

Capital Cost Recovery Rule

The target of allocation effort is one's cost or other basis. The term "cost" implies at time of acquisition. The term "other basis" implies a time after acquisition but before disposition. At time of disposition, the sale price must be allocated in such a way that the gain or loss for each asset sold can be determined correctly.

The key to cost allocation is to establish relative values of each asset at, or before, time of disposition. Unfortunately, many practical situations arise where value cannot be ascertained. When it is utterly impractical to do so, the rule of *capital cost recovery* prevails.

For example, suppose one acquired 100 units of A and 100 units of B for the lump sum cost of $10,000. A and B are nonlike assets so commingled at time of acquisition that their relative values could not be determined. Subsequently, the units were sold intermittently: 50 units B for $800; 50 units B for $1,200; and 30 units A for $3,000.

When the 100 B units are all sold, the owner will have recovered $2,000 of his $10,000 investment. This leaves $8,000 to be apportioned among the 100 A units. Thus, each A unit is allocated a cost of $80 per unit ($8,000 divided by 100 units). When the 30 units of A are sold for $3,000 (which is $100 each), there is a gain of $20 per unit ($100 minus $80) to be tax reported. When the other 70 units are sold, the amount of unit gain may be different, but the allocation of cost would remain the same: $80 per unit.

Suppose, now, that 100 units of A, 100 units of B, and 100 units of C were commingled and bulk purchased for $10,000. As above, consider that 50 units B were sold for $800 and 50 units B for $1,200. At this point, the owner would have recovered $2,000 of his investment. He still has A and C commingled such that he cannot determine their relative values.

He sells 30 units of A for $3,000. Thus, he has recovered $5,000 of his $10,000 investment. Subsequently, he sells 40 units of C for $5,000. He has now recovered his full $10,000. When this point is reached, the remaining units of A (70) and of C (60) are cost allocated at "zero" dollars each. Thereafter, whatever the A and C units sell for, the capital gain is the full sale price of each.

The capital cost recovery rule applies to multiple assets acquired in one bulk purchase, where relative values cannot be ascertained. A good example is the purchase of bulk assets in an "estate sale." The rule also applies to the interbreeding of assets from a single acquisition. It could apply, for example, to our introductory illustration: the rare painting and its display stand.

The rare painting was bought for $10,000. The photo rights were sold for $2,000; the reprint rights were sold for $3,000; and a 30% ownership share was sold for $5,000. At this point the initial buyer had recovered his full $10,000. Thereafter, each asset sold is allocated "cost zero."

An attempt to depict the capital cost recovery rule is presented in Figure 5.1. Caution: this rule is allowed only where the relative values of each separate asset cannot be truly ascertained. The burden of proving this impracticability is on the taxpayer.

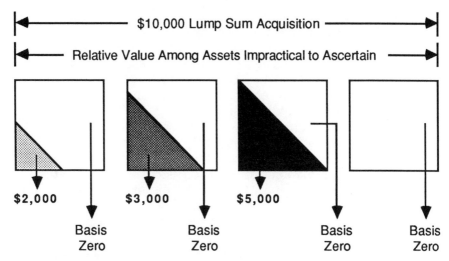

Note : $2,000 + $3,000 + $5,000 = $10,000 cost recovered

Fig. 5.1 - Concept of Capital Cost recovery Before "Zero Basis"

Equitable Apportionment Rule

It is not easy to prove that relative values cannot be ascertained. At some point, the *approximate* value of any asset is ascertainable. The asset itself does not have to be sold. Professional appraisers can be used; comparable sales can be used; replacement costs can be used; price bids can be solicited; and so on. The cost and time for doing so, however, may be prohibitive relative to the asset, or group of assets, being apportioned.

To illustrate the ascertainability aspects, consider that an investor buys a small farm at the distress price (arm's length) of $250,000. He does not intend to farm the land himself. He intends to sell the assets piecemeal for the best price that he can. He is seeking all of the capital gain/capital loss benefits to which he is entitled.

The farm consists of (1) land, (2) improvements to land (roadways, utilities, irrigation system, drainage, fencing), (3) producing trees (fruit and nut), (4) breed stock (horses and cattle), (5) farm buildings (workshop, stable, barn, pumphouse), (6) farm equipment (tractor, disc, fruit washer/sorter, jeep), and (7) a personal residence. Altogether, there are seven classes of property, each one a capital asset in its own right, and each subject to different tax rules. Proper allocation requires that each property class be cost-itemized in the purchase price of $250,000.

How does one go about making allocation of the gross cost?

The answer: A procedure called *equitable apportionment* of all assets in the gross cost. This generally means a concerted determination of the fair market value of each asset, or each class of assets, independently of the other assets.

The trick to equitable apportionment is to determine the fair market value of each asset or property class as though none of the others existed. If, in the example above, one obtains seven separate and distinct fair market values, each need bear no relationship whatever to the actual purchase cost. One may obtain fair value estimates from knowledgeable retailers, wholesalers, and brokers. When all seven market values have been separately ascertained, one adds them all up to a total market value. Suppose that this total comes to $385,000. This is quite different from the acquisition cost of $250,000.

"Step 1" in the allocation process is to identify and list each separate property class. Then associate a fair market value with each class. This is illustrated in Column 1 of Figure 5.2.

Developing reasonable market values for each property class is tedious, time-consuming, and frustrating. Most professional appraisers/estimators hedge their commitments. They give a range: high, low, and most probable. Before doing so, they want a detailed description of each asset within a class: its condition, age, model, species, and so forth. As unsatisfying as this effort is, it is better to undergo it pretax than post-tax. When one has a quarter-million-dollar investment at stake, some pretax frustration is preferable to inevitable post-tax apoplexy.

So, back to Figure 5.2.

"Step 2" in the allocation process is the fractioning of each property class in proportion to the total market value of all assets. This is done in Column 2 of Figure 5.2. Note that the numerator of each fraction is the market value of each class, whereas the

PROPERTY CLASS	Column 1 Market Value	Column 2 Fraction of Gross Value	Column 3 Cost Allocation
1. Farm land	100,000	$\frac{100}{385}$ = 0.2597	64,935
2. Land improv.	38,000	$\frac{38}{385}$ = 0.0988	24,675
3. Fruit trees	62,000	$\frac{62}{385}$ = 0.1614	40,260
4. Breed stock	50,000	$\frac{50}{385}$ = 0.1298	32,470
5. Farm buildings	28,000	$\frac{28}{385}$ = 0.0728	18,180
6. Farm equipment	45,000	$\frac{45}{385}$ = 0.1169	29,220
7. Residence	62,000	$\frac{62}{385}$ = 0.1606	40,260
TOTALS	385,000	$\frac{385}{385}$ = 1.0000	250,000

Fig. 5.2 - Equitable Apportionment With Estimated Market Values

denominator is the total market value of all classes. For accuracy, four-decimal-place fractions are used.

"Step 3" involves multiplying the gross acquisition cost ($250,000) by each fraction in Column 2. The final result in Column 3 is an allocation of cost that can withstand challenge and scrutiny by the IRS . . . years later.

Allocation Within a Class

What about the individual assets within each property class? The taxpayer/investor has the choice of repeating the process above for each item in a class, or using the capital-cost-recovery method for each class. Much depends on the magnitude of the cost allocations by class, and on the practicality of detailed itemization within each (tax) class.

For example, you go to a reputable auction house and buy a group of art sculptures in an estate sale. They are all works of art: either originals or limited editions. There are no duplicates. You pay $20,000 for five sculptures consisting of:

1. Hollow bronze dolphin (4 ft)
2. Welded-plate reindeer (3 ft)
3. Painted wooden horse (5 ft)
4. Wicker-wire spread eagle (3 ft)
5. Carved stone elephant (mid-size)

After paying your money and getting a receipt, you call a moving company. You freight them to a public storage facility where you have the sculptures insured, cleaned and repaired, and professionally appraised. The moving costs you $1,500; the insurance costs you $800 per year; the cleaning and repairs cost $600; the appraisal fee costs $1,000; and the storage costs are $150 per month. [Three years of storage and insurance comes to $7,800 (36 mo x $150 + 3 yrs x $800).]

After three years, you decide to sell. You contract with another auction house that has a large display pavilion. You call a moving company and have the five sculptures shipped to the pavilion. This costs you $2,000. The auctioneer contract gives the auction house a sliding commission on all sales made, plus 10% for overhead.

Being luckier than most sculpture collectors, the auction is a success. You receive a total of $36,000 net after commissions. The items sold as follows:

1.	Bronze dolphin	$ 1,500
2.	Welded reindeer	6,000
3.	Wooden horse	15,000
4.	Wire eagle	3,500
5.	Stone elephant	10,000
	Total sales price	$36,000

What is your allocated gain or loss on each item sold?

We summarize the results in Figure 5.3.

The very first line entries in Figure 5.3 are the appraised values shortly after purchasing the items. Since all items are of the same property class, the same appraiser does it all. You need these

COST ALLOCATION : BULK ACQUISITION "SAME CLASS" ITEMS						
	1.	2.	3.	4.	5.	
ITEM	Bronze Dolphin	Welded Reindeer	Wooden Horse	Wire Eagle	Stone Elephant	TOTALS
Appraised Value	2,500	5,000	10,000	5,000	6,000	28,500
Allocation Fraction	0.0877	0.1754	0.3508	0.1754	0.2107	1.0000
Purchase Cost	1,754	3,508	7,016	3,508	4,214	20,000
Appraisal & Repairs	140	281	561	281	337	1,600
Freight In & Out	307	614	1,228	614	737	3,500
Storage & Insurance	685	1,368	2,736	1,368	1,643	7,800
Cost Basis When Sold	2,886	5,771	11,541	5,771	6,931	32,900
Sales Price	1,500	6,000	15,000	3,500	10,000	36,000
GAIN or (LOSS)	(1,386)	229	3,459	(2,271)	3,069	3,100

Fig. 5.3 - Summary Data for Text Example of Auction Sale

independent values in order to allocate your costs at time of purchase. The per item allocation fraction then applies across-the-board to all holding costs. As you can see, storage and insurance costs start mounting up with holding time. If you expect to make any capital gain, you can't hold onto these sterile items indefinitely.

As the results in Figure 5.3 illustrate, you lost money on the bronze dolphin and wire eagle. You made money on the other three items, but not a killing. Since you put the art sculptures in storage and not in your home, you avert the IRS assertion that you made personal use of the items. Thus, you are a true investor and not a hobbyist. Your losses are fully tax recognized. These losses were useful in offsetting your gains. Otherwise, you'd pay tax on $6,757 (229 + 3,459 + 3,069) instead of on the $3,100 illustrated.

Allocation Among Fungibles

The word "fungible" means interchangeable. That is, certain assets are of such kind or nature that one specimen or part can be used in place of another specimen or equal part. The result is that any separate identity of individual assets is completely obscured. The assets become all "look-alikes."

In practice, fungible assets are not limited to those which are strictly similar and look-alike. Included are nonlook-alikes which are *tax like* in character. The allocation problems arise not so much because of their similarities or dissimilarities in size, shape, or looks. The problems arise because of cost uncertainties of those assets acquired over long periods of time: 5, 10, 15, or so, years. During the accumulation period, the assets are acquired irregularly and at widely differing prices.

For example, consider an investor whose goal is to acquire 100 North American 1-ounce gold bullion coins (American Eagle and Canadian Maple Leaf). These gold coins are similar in size, have distinctly different engravings and date stamps, and are priced exactly the same. They each contain exactly one ounce of bullion purity gold. You can hold several of these coins in one hand. They are easy to store in a safe-deposit box. Storage costs are modest: about $30 per year. Unlike the example of art sculptures above, storage costs alone are not going to drive the disposition timing.

Assume that over a period of 15 years, you bought two or three coins at a time, until you reached your goal of 100. You decided to sell them in batches of 25 coins, for the best price you can get. This means that you make four separate transactions. You kept all of your purchase receipts and safe-deposit-box costs. But you did not mark or flag the specific coins as you bought them. How do you cost allocate your coins at time of sale?

The answer is that one cannot do it with the allocation precision that the IRS would like. Arbitrary rules of convenience must be applied. These rules are:

1. The average cost rule.
2. First-in first-out rule.

3. Investor designation rule.
4. Last-in first-out rule.

All four rules require that the assets (coins) be logged chronologically when acquired, and chronologically when sold. This is for holding-period distinction purposes.

Fungible Rules Explained

Under the *average cost* rule, the total dollar amount in each holding-period category is divided by the total number of coins held. This gives an average unit cost per coin. If a specified number of coins is sold, the gain or loss is determined relative to the average cost. If the shortest holding period is greater than one year, you can disregard the holding-period distinction and use the average cost across the board.

Under the *first-in first-out* rule, you are required to identify the coins by acquisition blocks. An acquisition "block" may be yearly, quarterly, monthly, weekly, or daily. Much depends on your acquisitions through the overall period of accumulating the coins. For the 15-year period cited, a yearly acquisition block would be acceptable. The rule requires that the first year's batch of coins be sold before the second; the second year's batch before the third; and so on. All coins in an acquisition block must be sold at one time. Doing so means that the total cost of each block can be identified, and its relative gain or loss can be determined.

Under the *investor designation* rule, you can pick and choose among your acquisition dates or blocks. The chosen date or block, however, must be identified by documentation as to the number and cost of coins bought. You then take those specific coins and sell them. The advantage of this rule is that you can pick the date, batch, or block of coins of your choice, to give you the tax bias that you want. If you have a low tax year, you can pick among your capital gain coins. If you have a high tax year, you can pick among your capital loss coins.

The *last-in first-out* rule is an assertion by the IRS where a taxpayer/investor is negligent or indifferent towards Rules 1, 2, and 3. The presumption is that the last purchase is the first sale; the next-to-last purchase is the second sale; and so on. This is an accounting-backwards maneuver which maximizes the gross proceeds into short-term holding periods. This substantially reduces the benefits of long-term holding.

As an investor/taxpayer, you can select any of the fungible allocation rules that you want. But you must stick to your choice for each separate disposition event. You may use Rule 1 for coin batch A, Rule 2 for coin batch B, *and* Rule 3 for coin batch C. You cannot mix the rules for a given batch. That is, you cannot use Rule 1 *and* Rule 2 for coin batch B, for example.

Subdivision of Land

A variant of the fungible rules concept is raw land which has been subdivided for sale. Raw land is that which is either in its pristine state, or its surface has been worked nonextensively, or where some old buildings and trees have been removed and demolished. Such land is usually acquired in tract form consisting of a few acres to hundreds of acres. Depending on its particular location, the land may have much greater value when subdivided.

Today, most developable tracts of land where subdivision is likely are inherited by individuals rather than purchased. (We are addressing individual investors: not corporate entities or land development partnerships.) If inherited, the initial cost basis is the fair market value of the property in the decedent's gross estate for federal death tax purposes. [Tax code Sections 1014(a) and 2031(a).] It is up to the acquirer to obtain a copy of **Form 706**: U.S. Estate Tax Return, and to extract therefrom *Schedule A: Real Estate*.

The acquirer — if he intends to subdivide — then has to bear all the costs of getting the property surveyed, having it staked and partitioned into parcels, and making those improvements and impact studies as necessary for complying with local zoning ordinances. Instead of assigning the development costs to individual parcels, they are grossed into one's cumulative costs for prorata allocation. These cumulative costs include all developmental carrying charges, such as property taxes, mortgage interest, and liability insurance. For cost allocation purposes, all acres in the tract are treated as being uniform in unit content.

To illustrate the cost allocation aspects, consider that you acquired a 30-acre tract of raw land from a decedent family member. The fair market value of the land on Form 706 (Schedule A) was $160,000. As developable building sites, you were able to get a 5-year improvement loan (covering all development costs) of $380,000. During the five years of subdivision effort, the carrying charges amounted to $200,000. This gives you a total cumulative investment in the property of $740,000 (160 + 380 + 200).

After seemingly endless submission and resubmission of your development plans, the local planning commission finally authorizes 10 subdivision parcels. However, approval is conditioned upon dedicating 30% of all land to common areas (roads, easements) and open space. Because of variations in the surface terrain of the land, the minimum parcel size had to be no less than 2.5 acres and no more than 3.6 acres. Portions of the tract were flat land, and other portions had slopes, gullies, and knolls.

Using various assumed parcel sizes, the cost allocation effort is summarized in Figure 5.4. The amounts in the far right column represent the cost per parcel, at the time each is offered for sale. Although the unit cost per parcel is uniform, the sale price of each parcel will vary depending on its particular appeal to each buyer.

Accumulated Capital Cost = $740,000					
Unit Cost = $740,000 ÷ 30 Acres = $24,667 per Acre					
Parcel No.	Useable Acreage	Open Space	Total Acreage	Unit Cost	Cost per Parcel
	Acre	Acre	Acre	$/Acre	$
1	2.00	0.85	2.85	24,667	70,300
2	2.04	0.87	2.91	"	71,780
3	2.45	1.05	3.50	"	86,335
4	2.22	0.94	3.16	"	77,947
5	1.95	0.83	2.78	"	68,574
6	1.79	0.76	2.55	"	62,898
7	1.75	0.75	2.50	"	61,667
8	2.04	0.87	2.91	"	71,778
9	2.30	0.98	3.28	"	80,906
10	2.50	1.06	3.56	"	87,815
TOTALS			30.00		740,000

Fig. 5.4 - Illustration of Cost Allocation of Subdivided Land

Each Sale Must Close

Where capital investments are involved, allocation discipline is the prerequisite for determining the correct gain or loss upon disposition (sale) of each asset. However, no tax consequences flow until the disposition is closed. Disposition is the relinquishment of all dominion and control over the property held.

Ordinarily, a capital transaction is closed for tax purposes when there is a binding legal contract which unconditionally and irrevocably binds the parties to its terms. A binding contract generally arises when an offer by one party is accepted by another party, or by the agent thereof. It is a matter of applicable local law as to when acceptance takes place. When parties are in different jurisdictions (different states or foreign countries), conflict of acceptance laws may arise.

Acceptance must be bona fide and in good faith. Thus usually is signified by some specific, identifiable act. This act may be signature on a document, entry in official records, or some other third-party instrument with date and description thereon. Dated documentation is of utmost importance.

Portfolio brokers and managers function in terms of *trade dates*. These are legal business dates: 8 hours a day, 5 days a week . . . normally. Off-hours, weekends, holidays, and other announced closings are not legal trade dates. The trade dates and hours are those legal times when transactions are officially recorded on customer accounts at the home office. These dates and hours differ from instructional dates by investors and settlement dates by the financial institutions involved.

A closed transaction is accompanied by the *benefits and burdens* of ownership. Upon acquisition, the acquirer takes on all responsibilities for the property, exercises full dominion and control thereof, and enjoys the profits, if any, therefrom. The converse is true when the property is disposed of: the disposer ceases all dominion and control over it.

Closing a transaction is particularly important for sterile assets. This is because no current income is being generated to be reported to the IRS. As a result, the owner/seller is free to choose when to close and what to allocate. This freedom of choice permits you — the investor — to lead, lag, or coincide with a tax year to your best advantage.

6

PORTFOLIO ASSETS

Deriving Income While Holding Onto An Investment Can, At Times, Be Satisfying. But It Requires That You Thoroughly Understand The Use Of Schedule B (Form 1040). It Also Requires That You Read, Extract, And Understand The Many $-sign Boxes On Forms 1099-INT, 1099-OID, And 1099-DIV. If You Are A "Nominee Recipient," You have Certain Adjustments To Make (On Schedule B). The Instructions Tell You How To Report (Subtract) "Nominee Distributions." If You Engage In Automatic Reinvesting And Telephone Switching, You Have "Cost-When-Sold" Problems (On Schedule D).

By a wide margin, more money and wealth are placed in portfolio assets than in any other category of investments. There are several reasons for this.

Foremost, there is a wide diversity of portfolio instruments available for investment. There is diversity in amounts: from $100 or so to $100,000 or more. There is a diversity in underlying collateral: individual debtors, small businesses, real estate owners, financial institutions, and corporate giants. There is also diversity in location: local, national, and worldwide.

Being "paper" assets, portfolio instruments are easy to handle (by mail, phone, or computer), easy to record and file, and easy to safekeep. They are easy to originate, trade, exchange, and terminate. As paper instruments, they are backed by the "full faith and credit" of the issuer . . . whatever that means. Under some circumstances, the full faith clause is enforceable under state law.

Probably the most important reason for the popularity of portfolio assets is that they generate positive income while being held. Unlike sterile assets which generate no income, portfolio assets provide the holder with income of various tax forms. This income can be used by the investor to supplement his style of living, or may even constitute his sole source of livelihood. The idea that one can live in whole or part on income from his investments is indeed attractive and satisfying.

However, the fact that income is generated creates — or can create — capital accounting problems when a portfolio asset is disposed of. Not all investors understand or recognize their cost-when-sold problems. In this chapter, therefore, we want to address those issues of cost allocations which are aggravated by income during the holding period of assets. We also want to address the income reporting forms — the 1099 series — that we have not addressed previously. Income accounting and capital accounting require ongoing self-discipline by each investor involved.

Overview of Schedule B (1040)

Because current income is generated from portfolio assets, the one tax form that an investor will use year after year is Schedule B (Form 1040). The official heading on this schedule is: **Interest and Dividend Income**. An overview of its format and arrangement is presented in Figure 6.1. If you've been a portfolio investor before, we're sure that you have used this form more than once. Nevertheless, there are some special features concerning it that we want to tell you about.

As you are probably already aware, Schedule B (1040) consists of three parts, namely:

Part I   —   Interest Income
Part II   —   Dividend Income
Part III —   Foreign Accounts

A side note to Part I (on the official form) calls your attention to payer information returns: Forms 1099-INT and 1099-OID. Similarly, a side note to Part II calls your attention to Form 1099-DIV. We'll describe more fully below the payer information that goes on these 1099 forms.

Year	Your Name		Soc. Sec. No.
Form 1040	**Schedule B - Interest and Dividend Income**		
Part I	**INTEREST INCOME**		**Amount**
	1 . Personal lending arrangements List name of payer(s)	1	
	2(a). 1099 Payer reportings (gross) ● List name of payer(s) ● Separate entry for each 1099	2 (a)	
	2(b). Nominee, etc. adjustments ● List distributee(s) & Soc.Sec.No ● Explain Adjustments	2 (b)	< > < > < > < > < >
	3 . Enter total **on page 1** ▶ (after adjustments) **Form 1040**	3	
Part II	**DIVIDEND INCOME**		**Amount**
	4(a). 1099 Payer reportings (gross) ● List name of payer(s) ● Separate entry for each 1099	4 (a)	
	4(b). Nominee, etc. adjustments ● List distributee(s) & Soc.Sec.No. ● Explain adjustments	4 (b)	< > < > < > < > < >
	5 . Enter total (after adjustments) ⫸	5	
	6 . Capital gain distributions 6		
	7 . Nontaxable distributions 7		
	8 . Add lines 6 and 7 ⫸	8	< >
	9 . Enter total **on page 1** ▶ (after adjustments) **Form 1040**	9	
Part III	**FOREIGN ACCOUNTS**	**YES**	**NO**
	10(a). Any financial accounts in a foreign Country?		
	10(b). If "Yes", enter name of country _____		
	11 . Were you grantor of, or transferor to, a foreign trust?		

Fig. 6.1 - Edited General Format of Schedule B (1040)

The side note to Part III tells you to: *See instructions.* The instructions say—

Fill in this part if you had more than $400 of interest or dividend income; if you had a foreign financial account; or if you were the grantor of, or transferor to, a foreign trust.

Thus, if you earn more than $400 in (taxable) interest OR more than $400 in (taxable) dividends, you have to file Schedule B and check the "Yes-No" boxes in Part III.

A headnote to Part I reads, in part—

*If you received, **as a nominee**, interest that actually belongs to another person, or you received or paid accrued interest on securities transferred between interest payment dates, see [instructions].*

Similarly, a headnote to Part II reads, in part—

*If you received, **as a nominee**, dividends that actually belong to another person see [instructions].*

With respect to nominee matters, the instructions tell you to subtotal all amounts received, then enter the phrase: "Nominee Distribution(s)." List and name the redistributee(s), and subtract said amount(s) from the subtotal. You can also add other appropriate (subtraction) notations such as: accrued interest paid, tax-exempt interest, OID adjustment (original issue discount), and ABP adjustment (amortizable bond premium).

In other words, Schedule B recognizes your right to do whatever cost adjusting you need to in order to correct the capital accounting of your investments. In Parts I and II thereof, there are special lines and instructions to this effect.

Interest-Bearing Assets

The simplest form of portfolio investment is an interest-bearing asset. This is a "piece of paper" or "book entry" which, upon the investor advancing his money, entitles him to its full return when the instrument "matures." The instrument is a contract which states the amount of money (principal) loaned, the annual rate of interest, and a due date for return of principal. The due date can be extended by mutual consent between the parties.

Typical interest-bearing assets are passbook savings, money market accounts, certificates of deposit, commercial paper, promissory notes, trust deeds, revenue bonds, municipal bonds, corporate bonds, and so on. Also included are U.S.Treasury bills, notes, and bonds with varying length of maturity from 90 days to 30 years.

The tax accounting problem with interest-bearing assets is distinguishing between principal and interest. Each is taxed differently. It is surprising the number of investors who get confused over the difference.

If the instrument is interest-bearing only, with no payback of principal until maturity, the distinction between principal and interest is simple. The periodic payments received are pure interest income — fully taxable.

Where the periodic payments include a mixture of principal and interest, as is often the case, the investor has to keep track of his returned capital very diligently. Not all investors do this They assume that the borrower will keep track of the principal payback for them. This can be a mistake.

For example, suppose you lend $10,000 for a period of five years at 10% interest. To keep the monthly payments manageable, the principal is amortized over 15 years. Just before the end of the 5-year maturity date, you would have received approximately $2,500 in return of principal. On the 5-year due date, you would expect to receive the remaining $7,500. Your cumulative return of capital would be your original $10,000 (2,500 + 7,500). Therefore, no tax on the $10,000.

But, suppose that, at the end of five years, the borrower informs you that he has lost his job, or is going through divorce, or has filed bankruptcy, or (being an entity) is liquidating the underlying assets. Through legal counsel you manage to recover $2,000 principal on your remaining $7,500. Your legal fee was $500, which is subtracted from the $2,000. This gives you a net maturity recovery of $1,500. Now what is your situation?

You have a capital loss. Your loss is $10,000 minus your return of capital ($2,500 + $1,500). Thus, your net loss is $6,000. Although you might be tempted to claim so, your loss is not your original $10,000. You did recover some of it along the way.

All of which brings up a key distinguishing characteristic of interest-bearing assets. There is no likelihood of any capital gain whatsoever. The likelihood — hopefully remote — is capital loss. In order to claim this loss on Schedule D (1040), one has to diligently keep track of his return of principal all along the way. A potential loss is never made fully known until the maturity (demand) date of the interest.

Items on Form 1099-INT

Any and all interest income that you receive is reported to the IRS. It is reported by the **payer** on Form 1099-INT. When the IRS receives the interest information, it goes through exactly the same computer-matching procedure that we depicted back in Figure 3.2. As with those previously described 1099 forms in Chapter 3, the payer is required to furnish you a copy of the 1099-INT on or before January 31 each year.

What does Form 1099-INT look like? We're sure that you've seen one or more. Nevertheless, for instructional purposes, we present an edited/abbreviated version in Figure 6.2.

PAYER'S name, address & zip code		**YEAR** **FORM** **1099-INT**	**INTEREST INCOME**
		1. Earnings from savings, etc. $	
PAYER'S Tax I.D. No.	RECIPIENT'S Soc. Sec. No.	2. Forfeiture $	3. U.S. Bonds $
RECIPIENT'S name, address & zip code		4. Federal tax withheld $	
		5. Foreign tax paid $	6. Foreign country or U.S. possession

Fig. 6.2 - Edited/Abbreviated Version of Form 1099-INT

As you can note in Figure 6.2, there are *five* entry boxes on Form 1099-INT, each with a $-sign therein. Box 1 is for entering all forms of interest earnings other than Government bonds. The official description in Box 1 reads:

Earnings from savings and loan associations, credit unions, bank deposits, bearer certificates of deposit, etc.

The "etc." includes interest on life insurance dividends, delayed death benefits, homeowner association dues, mortgage impound accounts, and so on. However, Box 1 does not include interest derived from tax-exempt municipal bonds nor that from tax-deferred retirement plans.

In Box 2, the payer enters any interest or principal forfeited due to early withdrawals from time deposits. The forfeitures are not deducted from the entry in Box 1. Instead, they are deducted from one's total reported income on Form 1040 to arrive at one's "adjusted" gross income. When reviewing your Form 1099-INT, always look for any Box 2 forfeitures.

In Box 3, the payer reports separately all interest paid on U.S. Savings bonds, Treasury bills, Treasury notes, and Treasury bonds. The reason these items are reported separately is that federal government interest is not taxable income at the state level. The Box 3 income, however, is taxable at the federal level.

Boxes 4 and 5 on Form 1099-INT are for federal and foreign tax withholdings, if any. Although interest income is not normally subject to withholdings, there are situations where it is so. Examples are backup withholdings, alien withholdings, foreign source income, and direct instructions to the payer by the IRS.

All interest income is reported on Schedule B (1040): Interest and Dividend Income. Interest goes on the interest portion thereof (Part I), whereas dividends go separately on the dividend portion (Part II). Do not mistakenly enter your interest on the dividend portion of Schedule B. If you do, you'll be **computer taxed twice**: once for not entering it in Part I and again for erroneously entering it in Part II.

Items on Form 1099-OID

Another form of interest is "OID interest." The OID stands for: Original Issue Discount. This is the difference between the stated redemption price at maturity and the issue price of a debt instrument. The OID is like a bonus interest; it is paid up front to the first purchaser of a new debt issue. Frequently, the OID is in addition to regular interest paid periodically.

Prior to July 1, 1982, the amount of OID was treated as capital gain at time of maturity. But no more. As per Code Section

1272(a), all OID is included in current income on the basis of a constant interest rate. The annual inclusion is the total OID divided by the number of months from date of issue to date of maturity, times the number of months held during the taxable year.

The OID inclusion rule does not apply to maturity dates of one year or less. Nor does it apply where the total dollar discount is less than 1/4 of 1% of the stated redemption price at maturity, times the number of years to maturity.

For example, you buy from a reputable corporation a 10-year debt instrument which has a face value (at redemption) of $10,000. The original issue price is $9,800. Is the $200 OID includible on your tax return?

No, it is not.

The 1/4 of 1% of the stated redemption price is $25 [1/4 x 1% x $10,000]. This amount times 10 years comes to $250. Thus, the $200 discount is less than the $250 exemption amount.

However, if the OID amounted to $500, for example, the inclusion amount would be $4.16 per month or $50 per year.

How is the inclusion amount reported to the IRS by the payer? By another Form 1099 . . . of course. The applicable form is 1099-OID. It is completely separate from Form 1099-INT.

PAYER'S name, address & zip code		YEAR	ORIGINAL
		FORM 1099-OID	ISSUE DISCOUNT
		1. Current year OID $	
PAYER'S Tax I.D. No.	RECIPIENT'S Soc. Sec. No.	2. Other interest $	
RECIPIENT'S name, address & zip code		3. Forfeiture $	4. Federal tax withheld $
		5. Description	

Fig. 6.3 - Edited/Abbreviated Version of Form 1099-OID

Again, for instructional purposes, we present in Figure 6.3 an edited/abbreviated version of Form 1099-OID. As indicated therein, it contains four $-sign boxes. Box 1 is for the OID amount prorated for the current year; Box 2 is for other periodic interest, if any; Boxes 3 and 4 are self-explanatory.

If there is an entry in Boxes 1 *and* 2, there need to be two separate entries on Schedule B (Part I): Interest Income. The OID inclusion should be clearly so marked.

Because OID instruments are generally long-term debt: 10 to 40 years or so, an investor may sell his OID asset to some other investor. When he does so, he computes his capital gain or loss relative to his actual purchase price **plus** the cumulative OID that has been reported as income. Consequently, unless you hold an OID instrument to maturity, you need to keep track of your OID inclusions as part of your capital cost. Otherwise, you pay tax on the OID twice: once as income, and again as capital gain.

Using Schedule B: Part I

Referring back to Figure 6.1 for a moment, you see that there are three categories of entries in Part I: Interest Income. These categories are:

			$ Amount
1	—	Personal lending arrangements	_____
2(a)	—	1099 Payer reportings	_____
2(b)	—	Nominee, etc. adjustments	< >
3	—	Total of the above	_____

For Part I of the official form, there are approximately 12 entry lines. For multiple-asset investors, this number of lines is often insufficient for adequate tax accounting, particularly if several adjustments have to be made. Should this happen to you, add one or more "continuation" Schedules B and mark them respectively: B-1, B-2, B-3, etc. You must use a separate entry line, giving a brief identity of each person or entity who pays you interest.

An important caution: If you use more than one Schedule B (Part I) form, do your totalling on the very last continuation sheet. Do not subtotal on each Schedule B separately. In other words, leave line 3 blank on those sheets which are continued on the subsequent one. This way, the IRS computer will pick up only one total number rather than duplicating and triplicating everything that you have entered.

The instructions on Line 3 (Schedule B) direct your total to the line marked *Taxable interest income* on Page 1 of Form 1040. Once on Page 1 (1040), you can no longer make any adjustments for nominee distributions, accrued interest paid, tax-exempt interest, OID adjustments, or ABP (amortizable bond premium) adjustments. You must make all of your proper adjustments before transferring to Page 1 (1040) your total interest income.

Examples of how you use Schedule B (Part I) for making your subtractive adjustments are presented in Figure 6.4. You are urged to take all the lines and spaces that you need. Don't try to save paper or forms to help the IRS. Its computer is ruthless in its 1099 matching programs.

Sch. B	Part I	INTEREST INCOME	Year

Nominee, etc. adjustments	Amount
● Distributee A : Social Security No.	< >
● Distributee B : Social Security No.	< >
● Accrued interest paid to (name)	< >
● Tax-exempt interest (identify)	< >
● OID adjustment (identify)	< >
● ABP adjustment (identify)	< >
● Error on 1099 : (identify & explain)	< >

Where applicable, prepare Forms 1099-INT and 1099-OID; attach to Form 1096 (Transmittal) and send to IRS (address on back of Form 1096).

Fig. 6.4 - Candidate "Adjustments" on Schedule B (Part I)

Accrued interest, by the way, is when you buy a bond between its interest payment dates. You pay the accrued interest (before your ownership) to the person or entity who sold you the bond. You are allowed a subtraction on Schedule B for this.

Similarly, if an OID amount reported to the IRS differs from your actual holding accrual, you are allowed an OID adjustment. As always, you must identify and explain . . . with brevity.

If you pay a premium on a bond (which is the amount you pay in excess of its stated redemption value), you are allowed to amortize the premium over the holding period of the bond. Otherwise, when the bond matures, you only get its face value. If you have overlooked this premium, you should claim it on Schedule D as a capital loss.

Items on Form 1099-DIV

Compared to Forms 1099-INT and 1099-OID, Form 1099-DIV: **Dividends and Distributions**, is far more complicated. It consists of 10 — yes, 10 — data entry boxes. Of these 10 boxes, nine are labeled with $-signs. This means that there could be as many as nine different dollar amounts that must be accounted for on your return.

It would be most unlikely that all nine $-sign boxes on one given 1099-DIV form would be filled in. However, if you have multiple assets, each of which issues a separate 1099-DIV, you could easily have all nine $-boxes filled, two or three at a time on different 1099-DIV forms. This means that if you receive more than one Form 1099-DIV, as many portfolio investors do, you have to carefully examine each one, and mentally and physically record the cumulative amounts for each $-box designation. This is a preparatory accounting chore of its own.

The nine $-boxes of Form 1099-DIV are a source of endless confusion by investors. Although the boxes are officially labeled, it is not self-evident where the $-entries go on one's tax return. The confusion is aggravated because every investor knows the computer intransigence he faces with the IRS when trying to sort things out intelligently and reasonably.

Again, for instructional purposes, we present in Figure 6.5 an edited/abbreviated version of Form 1099-DIV. We have shown the 10 data boxes in their official sequence, but without their official numbers and headings. We particularly show the nine $-sign boxes. These are the ones that we want you to focus on.

Officially, the 10 boxes are designated as—

1. (1a) Gross dividends and other distributions on stock (Total of 1b, 1c, 1d, and 1e)
2. (1b) Ordinary dividends
3. (1c) Capital gain distributions
4. (1d) Nontaxable distributions

PAYER'S name, address & zip code	YEAR FORM 1099-DIV	DIVIDENDS AND DISTRIBUTIONS
	1. Gross dividends $	2. Ord. dividends $
PAYER'S Tax I.D. No. / RECIPIENT'S Soc. Sec. No.	3. Capital gains $	4. Nontaxables $
RECIPIENT'S name, address & zip code	5. Invest. expenses $	6. Fed. tax withheld $
	7. Foreign tax paid $	8. Foreign country or U.S. possession
	Liquidation Distributions	
	9. Cash $	10. Noncash $

Fig. 6.5 - Edited/Abbreviated Version of Form 1099-DIV

5. (1e) Investment expenses
6. (2) Federal income tax withheld
7. (3) Foreign tax paid
8. (4) Foreign country or U.S. possession
9. (5) Liquidation: Cash
10. (6) Liquidation: Noncash (Fair market value)

As officially stated in Box (1a), that $-entry is the total of Boxes 2 through 5 (1b, 1c, 1d, and 1e). This total figure (gross dividends) had better be on your tax return: Schedule B (Part II), Dividend Income. Furthermore, there should be a *separate* Box 1a entry on your Schedule B for **each** 1099-DIV **or substitute** issued to you. After these entries are made, it is then up to you to take advantage of any offsetting benefits on other lines, forms, and schedules of your return. As we tried to dramatize in Chapter 3: Broker Reportings, the IRS is only interested in your gross dividend income for its computer-matching purposes.

Using Schedule B: Part II

With so many $-sign boxes on Form 1099-DIV, you can readily understand the confusion that arises when trying to incorporate the paper-reported amounts on your own tax return. Although you must *start* with Schedule B (Part II), you may wind up using several other forms and schedules. We can best explain the problem(s) with a comprehensive example.

Assume that you receive three separate Forms 1099-DIV. You are not a nominee recipient, nor did you find any payer-reported errors on the 1099's. The Box 1 information contained on the three 1099's is as follows:

Item	DIV-1	DIV-2	DIV-3	Totals
Payer	ABC Corp.	DEF Corp.	GHI Corp.	
Box 1(a): Gross	$636	$219	$190	$1045
Box 1(b): Ordinary	500	150	20	670
Box 1(c): Cap-gain	None	50	165	215
Box 1(d): Nontax	112	14	None	126
Box 1(e): Expense	24	5	5	34
Box 1(a): Verify	$636	$219	$190	$1,045

The very first thing you do when receiving any 1099-DIV is to add up Boxes 1(b) through 1(e) to see if the total equals the amount reported in Box 1(a): Gross dividends. If not, Box 1(a) controls. This is what the IRS computer sees. You then adjust the other boxes (from whatever payer information you have) to conform to the Box 1(a) amount reported. Use "trial and error" procedures as necessary.

Once Box 1(a) and the sum of Boxes 1(b), 1(c), 1(d), and 1(e) equal each other, you enter the information on Schedule B (Part II). Using the data above, we've done this for you in Figure 6.6.

As illustrated in Figure 6.6., the three 1099-DIV gross dividends are reported in full. The total amount is $1,045. The two capital gain distributions of $215 plus the two nontaxable distributions of $126 become "adjustments." Therefore, they are *deducted* from the gross dividends to arrive at the net inclusion amount of $704 (1045 - 215 - 126). This inclusion amount goes on the line marked "Dividend income" on page 1 of your Form 1040.

As to the capital gain distributions (Box 1(c)), instructions preprinted on Schedule B (Part II) say—

Enter here and on Schedule D.

Sch. B	Part II	DIVIDEND INCOME	Year
LIST EACH 1099-DIV			**Amount**
DIV-1 : ABC Corp.			636
● C/G = None	■ N/T = 112		////////
DIV-2 : DEF Corp.			219
● C/G = 50	■ N/T = 14		////////
DIV-3 : GHI Corp.			190
● C/G = 165	■ N/T = None		////////
Total Gross Dividends ▶			1,045
● Capital gain distributions (C/G)		215	////////
■ Nontaxable distributions (N/T)		126	////////
Add These Adjustments ▷			< 341 >
Subtract Adjustments and Enter ➡			704
//////// Also Enter on Page 1, Form 1040 ———			▲

Fig. 6.6 - Example Entries on Schedule B (Part II)

If you look at Schedule D: Capital Gains and Losses, you'll find a line in Part II (long term) identified as—

Capital gain distributions.

Thus, Box 1(c) on Form 1099-DIV actually winds up on Schedule D, even though we initially reported it on Schedule B. On Schedule D, this part of your 1099-DIV can be used to offset any capital losses that you might have from other investments.

What happens to those other $-sign boxes on Form 1099-DIV? Particularly, what happens to Boxes 1(b), 1(d), 1(e), and 2: Federal income tax withholdings?

Please read on.

Other Amounts on 1099-DIV

As to Box 1(b): *Ordinary dividends*, you wind up paying full tax on them. There are no offsets. The only exceptions would be if you were a nominee recipient, or there was some obvious error in the reported amount. In this case, you may make the appropriate adjustments on Schedule B (Part II), similar to the adjustments shown in Figure 6.4 for Part I (Interest income).

As to Box 1(d): *Nontaxable distributions*, the official instructions leave you "hanging." All you're told is that Box 1(d) is deducted from gross dividends. After that, you are on your own. This means that you have to dig through the various confirmation statements that the payer sent you. You have to determine on your own which part of the Box 1(d) distribution is pure tax-exempt, if any, and which part is return of capital, if any. Any return of capital, recall, is not taxable.

There is so much confusion over nontaxable distributions. As a result, many investors simply deduct the reported amount(s) from the gross dividends on Schedule B (Part II), then promptly put the matter out of their minds. Technically, however, when you receive any return of capital as a dividend, you are supposed to adjust (reduce) your cost basis in the respective asset(s) to which the return of capital applies. On the other hand, if the dividend is pure tax-exempt, no reduction in basis is required.

As to Box 1(e): *Investment expenses*, you are left totally out on a limb. There are no official instructions to tell you what to do. Your presence of mind has to tell you that, somehow, being labeled as "expenses," it is deductible — or potentially deductible — somewhere on your tax return. Indeed it is. All of the Box 1(e) amounts on all of your Forms 1099-DIV are entered on Schedule A (1040) as: *Other Miscellaneous Deductions*. The Box 1(e) amount(s) arise when you are a shareholder in a nonpublicly-offered regulated investment company.

As to Box 2 on Form 1099-DIV: *Federal income tax withheld*, your first task is to check the corresponding federal withholding boxes on Forms 1099-INT and 1099-OID. (Recall Figures 6.2, 6.3, and 6.5.) Often, these federal withholding boxes are blank — but not always. So, check all of your 1099's carefully. Collect those showing federal withholdings, photocopy them, and **attach them** to your Form 1040 return. On page 2 of Form 1040, in the section headed: *Payments*, there is a line which reads—

Federal income tax withheld. If any is from Form(s) 1099, check ▶ ☐ .

If applicable, please "X" this little box on your 1040. If you do not, you lose payment credit for the $-amount(s) withheld. You probably have never even noticed this check-box before. In case you are not sure what we are talking about, take out your latest filed 1040, and look for it on page 2. Investors nationwide — and worldwide — lose hundreds of millions of dollars each year for not X-ing this box (when otherwise applicable).

The IRS's Form 1099 computer-matching programs are set to catch only your underreporting of gross interest and dividends: NOT underreporting your tax payments.

Foreign Accounts & Foreign Taxes

Investing today is a worldwide affair. It is not uncommon, and is often good investment strategy, to hold portfolio assets in countries other than the United States. You can acquire said assets directly by contacting foreign banks, foreign financial institutions, foreign brokerage houses, and other international intermediaries involved in foreign partnerships, trusts, and so on. Or, you can acquire foreign participation through mutual funds which themselves hold foreign assets in portfolio form. Either way, there are two particular tax matters of which you should be aware, namely: (a) Schedule B, Part III and (b) Foreign tax payments.

Part III of Schedule B is officially titled: Foreign Accounts and Foreign Trusts. There are two specific questions in this part which you must answer "Yes" or "No." We did not do justice to these two questions in our hasty overview of Schedule B in Figure 6.1. We cite now these two questions in full.

Question 1: At any time during [the taxable year], *did you have an interest in or a signature or other authority over a financial account in a foreign country (such as a bank account, securities account, or other financial account)?*

Question 2: Were you the grantor of, or a transferor to, a foreign trust that existed during [the taxable year], *whether or not you have any beneficial interest in it?*

If you answer "Yes" to Question 1, and the total value of your foreign investments exceeds $10,000, you have to file Form TDF 90.22-1. The title of this form is: Report of Foreign Bank and

Financial Accounts. Smack at the top of this form is your Social Security number. The purpose of this form, the instructions say—

is to assure maintenance of reports or records where such records or reports have a high degree of usefulness in criminal, tax, or regulatory investigations or proceedings.

If you answer "Yes" to Question 2, you have to read instructions and find out how to complete the following:

Form 926: Return by a Transferor of Property to a Foreign Corporation, . . . or Partnership

Form 3520: Creation of or Transfers to Certain Foreign Trusts

Form 3520A: Annual Return of Foreign Trust With U.S. Beneficiaries

In addition to Schedule B, Part III, there are those $-sign boxes on Forms 1099-INT and 1099-DIV labeled: *Foreign tax paid.* [Box 5 in Figure 6.2; Box 7 in Figure 6.5.] Most investor-sophisticated countries have tax treaties with the United States. The treaty arrangements are such that U.S. citizens or residents pay tax (through broker withholdings) on their foreign-earned interest and dividends to foreign governments, and, subsequent thereto, the investors can claim a tax credit on their U.S. returns. The amount of foreign tax paid is indicated on the Forms 1099. Claiming the foreign tax credit on Form 1040 requires still another form, namely: **Form 1116**: Computation of Foreign Tax Credit.

We are only trying to present to you the reality of investor life: USA. Investing in foreign countries provides you no relief whatsoever from the tax forms and capital accounting rules that we have discussed previously. Consequently, no matter where you invest your money these days, Big Brother — the IRS — is keeping a watchful eye on you.

Liquidation Distributions

There are two other $-sign boxes on Form 1099-DIV that we have not yet discussed. These are the last two boxes on the form titled: *Liquidation Distributions; Cash, Noncash.* These boxes apply only to shareholders in a corporation undergoing complete or partial liquidation. The instructions to the form specifically say—

Do not include this amount in Box 1(a).

Box 1(a), recall, is gross dividends which you must initially report on Schedule B, Part II. In other words, you do not use Schedule B for reporting liquidating distributions.

So, what are corporate liquidations and how are the distributions therewith handled on your tax return(s)?

A "liquidation" means that a corporation is going out of business, or is reorganizing/restructuring into an ongoing leaner business. In the process, the current shareholders must be distributed their prorata share of the former corporate assets. The distributions may be cash, noncash, or a combination of the two. The noncash may be reissued stock (in the reorganized entity), personal property (vehicles, furniture, equipment), accounts receivables, and fractional interests in real estate. When noncash is distributed, its fair market value on the date of distribution must be stated on Form 1099-DIV.

The liquidation distributions are treated as redemption sales or exchanges of stock in a former corporation. As a former shareholder, you report these redemptions on Schedule D (Form 1040). You report the redemption/liquidation value in Column (d): Sales price, in either Part I (short-term) or Part II (long-term), as appropriate. Then fill in all other appropriate columns in the subsection titled: *Other Transactions.*

Usually, in a corporate liquidation or reorganization, you are requested to turn in your old certificates to be cancelled. Whether you turn them in or not, they are canceled on the books of the former corporation. If stock in the reorganized entity is issued to you, that stock value goes on the books of the new corporation.

The net result is that you have participated — involuntarily, perhaps — in one or more capital transactions. In a liquidation or reorganzation, your canceled shares produce either a capital gain or capital loss on Schedule D. However, your new shares take on a "new start" cost basis equal to the Column (d) value reported on your Schedule D.

Automatic Reinvesting

In most cases, portfolio investors receive their dividend distributions quarterly. This includes ordinary dividends, capital gain distributions, and nontaxable (return of capital) distributions. This means that at least four dividend checks are received each year, for each batch of corporate shares held. If one has three corporate assets, for example, that's 12 dividend checks per year. If there are five corporate assets, that's 20 dividend checks per year. And so on. The more checks, the more confusion.

Most quarterly dividend checks are not of great dollar magnitude. They may range from less than $100 per check to maybe $500 or so. Nevertheless, some investors use these dividend checks to supplement their regular income.

Other investors, however, feel that receiving 10, 20, or more dividend checks a year is a nuisance. Each one has to be endorsed and deposited in some account or converted to cash. If they don't need these checks for everyday living, they instruct the payers to reinvest the dividends automatically. That is, instead of the investor receiving the actual checks and repurchasing additional shares, the payer does this automatically. This is a great convenience to both the payer and the recipient. In fact, it is too convenient. It lulls the investor into habitual oversight of his capital accounting.

Automatic reinvesting **increases the capital base** in each asset held. When the time comes to sell or exchange a particular asset, the capital cost basis is greater than the original investment. If the automatic reinvesting goes on for 5, 10, or more years, the reconstruction of capital additions four times a year becomes tedious and confusing. Most automatic reinvestors fail to keep track of their reinvestment contributions. The result is that — often — said reinvestors pay **triple tax** on their dividend income.

Let us illustrate the triple-tax situation.

Consider that you start with a $10,000 initial investment in a particular growth-income stock or mutual fund. You instruct the broker, payer, or manager to reinvest automatically all quarterly distributions. Assume that you hold the asset five years, and that during this period the annual distributions were as follows:

	Ordinary	Capital gain	Nontaxable
Year 1	300	120	50
Year 2	500	140	none
Year 3	180	360	160
Year 4	420	100	100
Year 5	260	60	300
Totals	1,660	780	610

After five years, you sell. What is your cost or other basis at time of sale? Assume that monetary inflation averaged 5% per year during each of your five holding-period years.

Answering the Above

You put in $10,000 initially. Over the five years, you received $610 in nontaxable distributions. This is "return of capital." Therefore, your initial investment as adjusted is $9,390 [10,000 - 610]. You are supposed to keep track of your nontaxable distributions and reduce your initial cost accordingly.

In five years, the purchasing power of your adjusted initial investment has been reduced approximately 25% due to inflation. Therefore, to compensate for this loss in money value, you need to "index" the $9,390 with a factor of 1.25. This converts your initial at-risk capital to $11,738 [9,390 x 1.25].

To this $11,738 figure, you add your total cumulative dividends that you automatically reinvested. This total is the sum of $1,660 in ordinary dividends, $780 in capital gain distributions, and $610 in nontaxable distributions. The total reinvestments come to $3,050 [1,660 + 780 + 610]. Altogether now, your capital investment at time of sale is $14,788 [11,730 + 3,050]. (Inflation indexing of annual dividends would not be accepted by the IRS.)

If you sold the asset for $10,000, you would have a capital loss of $4,788 [14,788 - 10,000]. Capital losses can be used on Schedule D to offset other capital gains.

If you sold the asset for $10,000 without keeping track of your automatic reinvestments, you would have neither a capital gain nor a capital loss. You invested $10,000 initially, and you got $10,000 back.

If you sold the asset for $15,000, you would have a capital gain of only $212 [15,000 - 14,788] — PROVIDED you kept track of your reinvestments. If you did not keep track, your Schedule D capital gain would be $5,000 [15,000 - 10,000].

By not keeping track of your automatic reinvestments, you pay the *triple tax*. You pay ordinary tax each dividend year. You pay an "inflation tax" on your initial investment. You pay a capital gain tax at time of sale. If you like paying taxes this much, the IRS will love you . . . but will not thank you.

If you have multiple dividend-paying assets, and you hate the tedium of automatic reinvestment accounting, there is a pleasant alternative. You can deposit, assign, or automatically transfer ALL of your quarterly dividends to a common money-market *checking* account. You treat this account as your ongoing "capital accounting ledger." The arrangement that we have in mind is depicted in Figure 6.7. You might want to take a moment to trace through the money flows indicated.

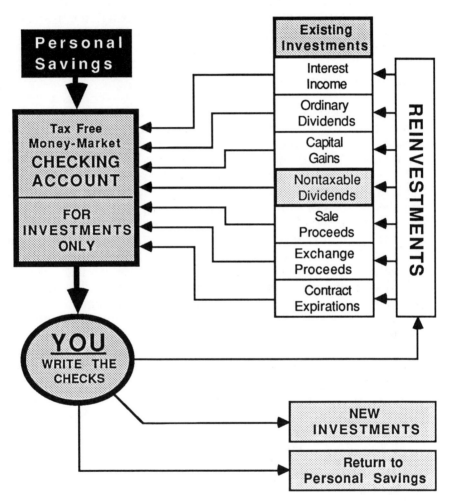

Fig. 6.7 - "Capital Accounting Ledger" for Portfolio Assets

All dividends — as well as all transaction proceeds — go into your **one** investment checking account. (It is even possible to set up a *tax-free* money-market checking account. Ask your investment broker or mutual fund manager about this.) If you want to do any reinvestments or make new investments, you simply write a check for any whole-dollar amount. It is easier to keep track of the investment checks that you write than to dig through the avalanche of computer printouts that brokerage firms and mutual funds send when confirming your automatic reinvestments.

Telephone Switching

The telephone, computer, and electronic transfer authorizations make it so easy to switch money from one investment asset to another. In fact, some portfolio investors enjoy this activity immensely. It is called "telephone switching" of investments. The objective is to try to beat the market averages by not investing and holding for substantial periods of time. Rarely does a telephone switcher hold on to an investment more than a year.

Telephone switching can become addictive and hypnotic. In the chase for gain, it is easy to get carried away. In the excitement, one overlooks the fact that each and every switching transaction is a SEPARATE tax accounting event. When you "switch in," you must establish your capital cost at that moment. When you "switch out," you must establish your gain or loss for that transaction.

It makes no difference that the in-out round trip lasts only one day, one week, one month, or whatever. It makes no difference that you never see the money in your hands or in your checkbook. Every in-out cycle must be tax accounted for on its own. You cannot simply aggregate your cumulative switchings for the year, and report only the net capital gain or net capital loss. This is the reasonable thing to do, but it is too easy. The IRS's matching computer vehemently objects to any aggregation.

If you are an habitual telephone-investment switcher, we strongly urge that you get in a supply of **Schedule D-1**'s: Continuation Sheet for Schedule D (Form 1040). Recall our discussion in Chapter 4 with regard to Schedule D/D-1, and particularly Figure 4.2 for the entries required. Keep a D-1 beside your telephone at all times. When you switch out of an investment, complete the tax accounting details at that time. Otherwise, if you wait until tax filing time, the pressure of filing will cause memory blocks and oversights.

7

CONDUIT ASSETS

> Your Most Important Tax Attention To Conduit Investments Hinges On Entity-Prepared Schedule K-1's And Your Schedule E (1040). There Is A K-1(1065) For Limited Partnerships, A K-1(1120S) For S-Type Corporations, And A K-1(1041) For Business Trusts. From These "Information Returns," The IRS Selects The Positive Income And Capital Gain Data For Its Computer Matching. Your Pass-Through Credits And Deductions Are Computer Ignored. Your Ability To Claim (On Schedule E) Your Distributive Share Losses Is Limited By "At-Risk" Rules (Form 6198) And "Passive Activity" Computations (Form 8582).

Portfolio assets generate positive current income in most cases: never negative. In contrast, conduit assets may — and often do — generate negative current income (loss). This negative income may be used to offset other positive sources of income on an investor's tax return. It is for this reason, among others, that conduit assets are favored for tax sheltering and tax planning endeavors.

A conduit asset is a business entity which is managed by someone other than the investor himself/herself. The underlying business may be any endeavor where there is a profit motive . . . at the end of the tunnel. In the process of seeking that profit, all income — positive or negative — and certain credits and deductions are "passed through," prorata, to each individual investor. It is then up to each investor to enter the designated pass-through amounts on the proper lines, forms, and schedules of his own tax return.

The pass-through (conduit) information is reported to investors on **Schedule K-1's**: [Investor's] Share of Income, Credits, Deductions, Etc. There are three of these K-1 information returns, namely:

Sch. K-1 (1041)   —   for Beneficiaries of Trusts
Sch. K-1 (1065)   —   for Partners in Partnerships
Sch. K-1 (1120S)   —   for Shareholders in S Corporations

As well as being reported to each investor, the same information is electronically reported to the IRS.

In this chapter, we want to focus on the kinds of information reported on the K-1's, and explain their extraction and entry onto your own tax return. Our basic model for instructional purposes will be Schedule K-1 (Form 1065) for partnerships.

Types of Partnerships

Section 761(a) of the Internal Revenue Code defines a "partnership" as—

*a syndicate, group, pool, joint venture, or other **unincorporated** organization through or by means of which **any business**, financial operation, or venture is carried on, and which is **not** . . . a corporation or a trust.* [Emphasis added.]

In our context, therefore, a partnership is any association of investors who, as a group entity, engages in a bona fide active business. It is not necessary that all individual partners themselves participate in the business, so long as there are designated managers to run the business and report annually to each partner his or her "distributive share" of the business.

Except for portfolio investments and holding-company passivity, there are no restrictions on the type of business that a partnership may engage in. The business may be farming, fishing, mining, oil and gas, timber harvesting, real estate, sales, rentals, manufacturing, movie films, art galleries, book publishing, and so on. This diversity of qualified businesses means that the distributive share items to each partner/investor will also be diversified.

There are three types of partnerships, namely:

• General partnerships,
• Limited partnerships, and
• Master limited partnerships.

In a general partnership, two or three, maybe five, persons get together to operate a business. Each contributes money, property, experience, and personal time. As a consequence, each general partner has a direct say in the management of the business. The focus in this chapter is **not** on general partnerships.

A limited partnership is a group of investors — 100 or so, or more — who do not themselves participate in the daily operation and management of the business. They agree to, or majority-designate, one or more general partners to run the business. When organized under applicable state law, limited partners have no direct say in the operation of the business. For this, their legal liability is limited to the extent of their invested capital and any personal (recourse) indebtedness they may assume on behalf of the partnership. Most limited partnership interests are privately solicited.

A master limited partnership (MLP) is a limited partnership in which the general partner and manager is a corporate entity. The corporate entity defines the business purpose and goals, then "packages" the partnership interests into *MLP units* of some par value. After registering the MLP units with state and federal securities agencies, the units are offered to the general public like shares in a corporation. The business, however, operates as a partnership with pass-through distributive share features.

Overview of Schedule K-1 (1065)

There is one central feature of every legally recognized partnership. The partnership entity itself is not subject to income tax. The individual partners are. Code Section 701: **Partners, Not Partnership, Subject to Tax** says very clearly that—

A partnership as such shall not be subject to the income tax. . . . Persons carrying on business as partners shall be liable for income tax only in their separate or individual capacities.

The only way that individual partners — the limited partners particularly — know what their tax accounting liabilities are is by some *information return* submitted to them by the general partner(s). The particular information return of interest here is **Schedule K-1**

(Form 1065). The official title of this form is: Partner's Share of Income, Credits, Deductions, Etc. This K-1 form itself contains no computation of tax. It simply lists those distributive share items which apply to each investor/partner.

For overview purposes, we present in Figure 7.1 a highly edited and condensed version of Schedule K-1 (1065). The official form actually takes two full pages. Excluding the head portion, there are approximately 50 — yes, 50 — separate entry lines on a partnership K-1. No wonder many investors' eyes "glaze over" when receiving their K-1.

The official instructions describing the purpose of Schedule K-1 say—

> *The partnership uses Schedule K-1 to report your share of the partnership income, credits, deductions, etc. **Please keep it with your tax records. Do not file it with your tax return.** A copy has been filed with the IRS.*
>
> *You are liable for tax on your share of the partnership income, whether or not distributed, and you must include your share on your tax return.*
>
> *The amount of loss and deduction that you may claim on your tax return may be less than the amount reported on Schedule K-1. **It is the partner's responsibility to consider and apply any applicable limitations.***

These official instructions put you on notice that you have to read the K-1 and do some homework. So, please take a moment, unglaze your eyes, and read through the features of Figure 7.1. We think we've simplified that K-1 quite admirably. Fortunately, rarely are more than five or ten entry lines applicable to a limited partner.

S Corporations & Trusts

S corporations and estates and trusts also issue Schedule K-1's. The S corporation K-1 (1120S) is quite similar in arrangement to Figure 7.1. It has the same number of entry lines (about 50), but they are titled differently in some instances. The few line title differences are due to tax accounting differences between partnerships and corporations.

Sch. K-1 Form 1065	PARTNER'S DISTRIBUTIVE SHARE ITEMS	Tax Year
Partner's Soc.Sec.No.	**Partnership's Fed.I.D.No.**	

Name & address of partner	Name & address of partnership
Questions, liabilities, & checkboxes ☐ ☐	Questions, percentages, & checkboxes ☐ ☐

Partner's Capital Account

Pass-through Item	Amount	Forms
Income (Loss) 12 items		Sch. B (1040) Sch. D (1040) Sch. E (1040) Form 4797
Deductions 4 items		Sch. A (1040)
Credits 7 items		Form 3800 Form 5884 Form 6765
Self-Employment 3 items		Sch. SE (1040)
Tax Preferences 7 items		Form 6251
Investment Interest 3 items		Form 4952
Foreign Taxes 5 items		Form 1116
Investment Credit Recapture 7 items		Form 4255
Other Items & Elections as provided by partnership		Form 4136 Form 8283 Form 8308 Form 8586

Fig. 7.1 - Abbreviated Contents of Schedule K-1 (Form 1065)

An S corporation is a private entity consisting of 35 or fewer shareholders, all of whom are U.S. citizens or residents. The stock is of "book entry" type which cannot be publicly traded. The letter "S" stands for "small business corporation" which is defined by Section 1244(c)(3) as an entity whose shareholders' capital does not exceed $1,000,000 (1 million).

S corporations generally operate at a loss initially. This makes them attractive to entrepreneurial investors. The shares can be designated as "Section 1244 stock," which makes any disposition losses writeoffable as ordinary loss rather than capital loss. S corporations are ideal for starting up a new business which, if successful, can be converted to a full-fledged C corporation paying dividends. The tax rules on S corporations are prescribed in Sections 1361 through 1379 of the tax code.

An estate or trust K-1 (1041) has about 30 entry lines. Of this number, about 10 are devoted to depreciation, depletion, and amortization of rental realty, equipment rentals, mineral resources, farming operations, and other business property. The K-1 (1041) has many fewer pass-through credits and deductions than those in Figure 7.1. However, capital gains and capital losses do pass through similarly.

Most estates and trusts are characterized as "family businesses." The five to ten or so beneficiaries (investors ?) are spouses, children, grandchildren, brothers, sisters, etc. It is doubtful that any outside investor could buy into such activities. However, there are commercially available business trusts which offer investors the pass-through benefits of real estate, mineral resources, mortgage backed securities, and commodity trading.

Problems With All K-1's

There are recipient problems with all K-1's. Problems prevail whether the conduit entity is a partnership, S corporation, or trust. Specifically, the problems are—

1. Use of substitute forms,
2. Issued late in the tax season, and
3. Numerous ancillary forms.

As to Problem 1, the preparers of the K-1's (the entity managers) are allowed to use their own substitute forms. There are no standard substitutes. The obvious reason is that some entities need to make only one or two entries; others may need to make five or six or so. Different issuing entities use different computers, different accountants, and different tax laws. The only standardization requirement is that the entries on the substitute forms must exact-match the line numbers on the official K-1 forms. If you are a multiple K-1 recipient, our suggestion is: Get the official K-1 form(s) for your conduit asset(s), and use each for cross-referencing the substitutes. Otherwise, you could make errors when extracting the K-1 data from the substitutes and transferring it to your return. The official K-1's and their instructions direct you to the correct schedules and lines on your own return.

As to Problem 2, the K-1 preparers are not required to issue them to you until April 15 each year. The result is that almost invariably you are forced to file your return late. To avoid this, we suggest that you contact each conduit manager no later than March 1 and request your K-1 information by phone or fax. Have an official K-1 handy so that you can transcribe the voice or fax information onto it.

As to Problem 3, there are some 15 to 20 ancillary forms that you may need for attaching to your own return. In Figure 7.1, we list 18 of these forms and schedules (almost the same number for S corporations, but fewer number for trusts). The 1040 Schedules A, B, D, and E come with your official tax forms package in January. But as to most of the other forms in Figure 7.1, you have to request them from the IRS Forms Center nearest you.

To add to the multiplicity of forms problem, the instructions tell you that if there are any errors on the K-1's, any nominee reportings, any inconsistent data, or any nonreceipt of a K-1, there is another form for you. It is **Form 8082**: Notice of Inconsistent Treatment. If you have more than one K-1 entity reporting on you, we urge that you have several Forms 8082 on hand. The mere existence of the 8082 form implies that computer-matching the entity prepared K-1's with your return is a nightmare for the IRS.

The K-1 Head Portions

The first step for averting IRS computer harassment is to read carefully the head portion of each K-1 that you receive. Whether investing in a partnership, an S corporation, or a trust, there are two large side-by-side spaces at the head. The left-hand block displays your (the recipient's) identifying number (social security); the right-hand block displays the entity's identifying number. Each ID number consists of exactly nine digits. If you get the entity's ID number correct when reporting the K-1 data on your own return, your computer-matching concerns will ease materially.

Partnership and S corporation K-1 head portions also include check-boxes, entry spaces, $-signs, and %-signs. In each case, a key reference check-box date is October 22, 1986. This is the date after which drastic changes in the tax laws affecting conduit assets became effective. On the partnership K-1, your percentage of profit sharing, loss sharing, and ownership of capital are shown. On the S corporation K-1, your percentage of stock ownership is shown, plus any "shareholder-day" changes during the year. You should look for and mentally record your ownership percentages.

On the partnership K-1, there is an Item J titled: Analysis of Partner's Capital Account. This analysis (as rearranged) consists of seven columns of dollar amounts. So important is this portion for capital reconciliation purposes that we present it in full in Figure 7.2. On the official K-1, the columnar headings are in small print and difficult to read. On preparer substitute forms, the columnar headings are abbreviated almost to the point of being meaningless.

Please read through Figure 7.2 carefully. It tells you in succinct form what took place in the partnership throughout the year, in your behalf. The really important item is the amount of your capital account at the end of the partnership tax year. You probably know the amount you originally invested. But do you know the amount of your investment at the end of your K-1 year? You'll find the answer in Column (g) of the reconciliation account.

Distributive Share Income

When addressing conduit assets, the term "income" also includes the term "loss." That is, the reportable income can be either positive or negative. We mentioned this earlier. The partnership and S corporation K-1's recognize this feature by using the combined phrase: *income (loss)*. (Trusts don't pass through losses very often.)

When showing negative income on a K-1 (or on your own tax return, for that matter), the amount is indicated by its enclosure in parentheses ( ) or brackets < >. Some professional and entity computers use the minus sign (-), but this sign is too easily overlooked on tax forms. Consequently, if the ( ) or < > are not expressly shown, the IRS computer reads the amount as positive and taxes you accordingly. This is NOT a trivial point, believe us. The IRS matching computers are set only to read positive income:

Sch. K-1 Form 1065	ANALYSIS OF PARTNER'S ACCOUNT		Item J
Col.	**Money Summary**		**Amount**
(a)	Capital account at beginning of year	▶	
(b)	Capital contributed during year	▶	
(c)	**Income (loss) from lines 1, 2, 3, and 4***	▶	
(d)	Income not included in Column (c), plus nontaxable income	▶	
(e)	Losses not included in Column (c), plus unallowable deductions	▶	< >
(f)	Withdrawals and distributions	▶	< >
(g)	Capital account at end of year. Combine Columns (a) through (f)	➡	
	* See Fig. 7.3		

Fig. 7.2 - Investors "Capital Accounting" on Schedule K-1 (1065)

not the negative. Negative income does not produce tax revenue for Big Government.

In our Figure 7.2, Column (c): Income (loss) makes reference to "lines 1, 2, 3, and 4." These are official line numbers on the partnership and S corporation K-1's. It is appropriate now that we reveal to you what kind of income (loss) these lines anticipate. We do so in Figure 7.3. Note that line 4 consists of six sub-lines: 4a through 4f. Also note that we have added lines 5, 6, and 7 which show on the official K-1 (1065).

Particularly note in Figure 7.3 its Column (c). As a Form 1040 filer, it alerts you to the specific schedules on **your return** that you must use. On some lines, the Column (c) entry says—

See Partner's Instructions for Schedule K-1 (Form 1065)

These K-1 (1065) instructions consist of eight pages of three columnar small print text. When skimming any official instructions, always look first for the bold-printed matter.

Partner's Soc. Sec. No.		Partnership's Fed. I.D. No.

Caution: Refer to Partner's K-1 Instructions before entering from this schedule on your Form 1040 tax return

INCOME (LOSS) (a) Distributive Share Item		(b) Amount	(c) Enter amount in Column (b) ON:
1	Ordinary income (loss) from trade or business		Schedule E, Part II
2	Net income (loss) from rental realty		Schedule E, Part II
3	Net income (loss) from other rental activities		Schedule E, Part II
4	Portfolio Income (Loss)		
a	● Interest		Schedule B, Part I
b	● Dividends		Schedule B, Part II
c	● Royalties		Schedule E, Part I
d	● Short-term capital gain (loss)		Schedule D, Part I
e	● Long-term capital gain (loss)		Schedule D, Part II
f	● Other portfolio income (loss)		Schedule E, Part IV
5	Guaranteed Payments		Schedule SE, Part I
6	Net gain (loss) under Section 1231		Form 4797
7	Other income (loss) (Attach Schedule)		Form 4684

Fig. 7.3 - Income Items Reported to IRS on K-1 (1065)

Lines 1 through 4f, we believe, are self-explanatory in Figure 7.3. Line 5 is for compensation to the general partner(s), and for guaranteed payments to limited partners, if so stipulated in the partnership agreement. Line 6 reflects gain (loss) from the sale of partnership assets, called "Section 1231" sales. These sales are reported by you on Form 4797: Sales of Business Property. This form directs your gain to Schedule D (1040) and your loss to a separate line on page 1 of Form 1040.

Line 7 (in Figure 7.3) is a catchall for other miscellaneous forms of income (loss), such as casualties and thefts. The instructions list other types of income or (loss). You are warned, however, that your losses may be — and usually are — severely limited.

Other Items on the K-1's

In addition to the income (loss) items in Figure 7.3, there are numerous other items on the K-1's (1065, 1120S, and 1041). Most of these items are credits, deductions, allowances, investment interest expenses, certain tax preferences, foreign taxes paid, and other adjustment matters. There are simply too many of these items for meaningful instruction here.

Instead of leaving you high and dry, we are listing below (in numerical order) the applicable ancillary forms involved. If you want to claim all of your tax credits, deductions, etc., you need to complete one or more of the following forms:

- 1116 — Computation of Foreign Tax Credit
- 3468 — Computation of Investment Credit
- 3800 — General Business Credit
- 4136 — Computation of Credit for Federal Tax on Fuels
- 4562 — Depreciation and Amortization
- 4684 — Casualties and Thefts
- 4797 — Sales of Business Property
- 4952 — Investment Interest Expense Deduction
- 5884 — Jobs Credit
- 6478 — Credit for Alcohol Used as Fuel
- 6765 — Credit for Increasing Research Activities
- 8283 — Noncash Charitable Contributions
- 8586 — Low-Income Housing Credit
- 8801 — Credit for Prior Year Minimum Tax

What is the purpose of all of these forms?

To answer the question, we have to let you in on a little secret. Because all credits, deductions, allowances, etc. **reduce** your income tax liability, they are NOT COMPUTER MATCHED by the IRS!

The IRS computer matches only the positive income and gross proceeds reported on your various K-1's. These items favor the government. Anything in your favor is computer overlooked. To discourage and intimidate you from claiming those items in your favor, you must work your way through the barricade of tax forms above.

Your Schedule E (1040)

There is one reporting schedule that attaches to your Form 1040 that we have not yet discussed. This is Schedule E (1040): **Supplemental Income and Loss**. The headnote below its main title reads—

From rents, royalties, partnerships, S corporations, estates, trusts, REMICs, etc.

This variety of investment activities certainly explains the word "supplemental" in its title.

Schedule E (1040) is organized into four parts, namely:

Part I   — Income or Loss From Rentals and Royalties
Part II   — **Income or Loss from Partnerships and S Corporations**
Part III — Income or Loss From Estates and Trusts
Part IV   — Income or Loss From Real Estate Mortgage Investment Conduits (REMICs)

We'll defer comment on Part I until the next chapter (Chapter 7: Rental Real Estate). Our focus here is primarily on Part II: Partnerships and S Corporations. Some of the aspects of Part III are reflected in Part II. Part IV is a hybrid of partnership and portfolio matters, analogous to Part II.

Part II of Schedule E is partitioned into two side-by-side portions. The left portion is titled: *Passive* Income and Loss; the right portion is titled: *Nonpassive* Income and Loss. The term "nonpassive" applies to general partners, managers, consultants, trustees, and others who participate in active conduct of the entity trade or business. Most of these participants pay the social security tax. The term "passive" applies to investors, who simply put their money in and hope for the best. With these comments in mind, we present in Figure 7.4 an edited and rearranged version of Part II (Schedule E) for passive investors.

As you can see in Figure 7.4, most of the entry-line spaces are for identifying your investment entities. Those which are foreign must be check-mark indicated. Each entity must be described on a

Schedule E Form 1040	SUPPLEMENTAL INCOME AND LOSS		Year Page 2

Your name		Soc. Sec. No.

Part II	**Partnerships and S Corporations**

If loss is from an "at-risk activity", is the -	**(e)** All at risk	
Investment At Risk? If (f) attach Form 6198	**(f)** Some at risk	

	(a) Name of Entity	**(b)** P or S ?	**(c)** Foreign ?	**(d)** Entity ID No.
A				
B				
C				
D				
E				

	(g) Loss Allowed (Form 8582)		**(h)** Positive Income (Schedule K-1)
A		A	
B		B	
C		C	
D		D	
E		E	
	Totals ➡	< >	Totals ➡
	Combine totals of Columns (g) and (h) ▶		

Fig. 7.4 - Edited Rearrangement of Schedule E (1040), Part II

separate line of its own, together with its 9-digit ID number and either the symbol **P** (for partnership) or **S** (for S corporation). The positive income generated by an entity, as reported to you on its Schedule K-1, can be entered directly into Column (h). No recourse to other forms is required.

Each Schedule E (Part II) is designed to accommodate five pass-through entities only. If you have more P and S entities than this, add *continuation* Schedule E's. Mark them E-1, E-2, E-3, and so on. When you do so, strike out the repetitive A, B, C lettering and continue it in alphabetical sequence on the added schedules. As always with continuation sheets, you should show your subtotals and combined totals on the very last scheduled form.

Passive Loss Limitations

If your P and S entities K-1 report negative income (loss), you are confronted with two auxiliary forms before making any entry in

Column (g) in Figure 7.4. The first of the two forms is **Form 6198**: At-Risk Limitations. The second is **Form 8582**: Passive Activity Loss Limitations. You must consider Form 6198 before going on to Form 8582.

At the very head of Part II (Schedule E), there is a caution which reads—

> *If you report a loss from an at-risk activity, you MUST check either column (e) or (f) to describe your investment in that activity. See instructions. If you check column (f), you must attach Form 6198.*

Columns (e) and (f) are headed: **Investment at Risk?**

(e) *All is at risk* ☐

(f) *Some is at risk* ☐

Section 465(c) of the tax code defines "at-risk activities" as those engaged in—

(A) holding, producing, or distributing motion picture films or video tapes,

(B) farming (the cultivation of land or the raising or harvesting of any agricultural or horticultural commodity including the raising, shearing, feeding, caring for, training, and management of animals),

(C) leasing of equipment and facilities other than real estate,

(D) exploring for, or exploiting, oil and gas resources, or

(E) exploring for, or exploiting, geothermal deposits.

If your P or S entity is not engaged in these activities, you can leave columns (e) and (f) blank. However, to be on the computer-safe side, it is best to check-mark Column (e): All is at risk.

If your P or S entity is engaged in one of the above cited activities, you are at risk to the extent of your cash investment plus borrowed money (for which you are personally liable for repayment), plus contributed property (which is free and clear). You are **not** at risk for any *nonrecourse* loans which the entity may have obtained for its asset acquisitions and operations. Nonrecourse loans are borrowed amounts (cash or property) for use by the entity which are not secured by your own property, which are protected against loss by a guarantee, or which are advanced by close family members. If your P or S entity has any nonrecourse loans, then you have to check-mark Column (f): Some is not at risk.

If you check Column (f), you have to complete and attach Form 6198: At-Risk Limitations. This form is not the model of simplicity and clarity that one would like. You'll definitely need professional assistance.

Once you get past Form 6198, your next attachable item is Form 8582: Passive Activity Loss Limitations. This form and its instructions are a little easier to follow. In fact, the loss allowability concept is quite simple. Your aggregate losses (negatives) are allowable to the extent of your aggregate incomes (positives). Those losses in excess of your incomes are disallowed . . . for the current year. Your unallowed losses may be carried forward to the next succeeding year or years, to offset any positive incomes in those years.

Sale, Exchange, Termination

Sooner or later, most investors terminate their conduit interests. When they do so, the disposition is treated as a Schedule D (1040) matter: Capital Gains and Losses. A conduit interest is a capital asset just like sterile and portfolio assets. BUT, there are significant differences at time of disposition.

The first disposition difference is that, except for master limited partnerships, conduit interests are not publicly traded. This means that you first have to contact the general partner (of a limited partnership) or the general manager (of an S corporation). You advise him of your desire to dispose of your interest and request that he make inquiry to other partners and shareholders. These persons have contractual rights of "first refusal." If there are no takers among the entity investors, you may then make private arrangements on your own.

The second disposition difference is that your conduit asset is probably not worth very much after several years of holding it. Chances are, you have used up all, or most, of the pass-through tax benefits to which you were entitled. If so, there's not much value left to sell or exchange. If, for example, you put up $10,000 initially and over the years wrote off, cumulatively, $9,000 in tax benefits, you can't expect to get your full $10,000 back. Any interested buyer is going to want to see your tax returns in order to reconstruct the writeoffs that you have taken. You will be expected to go through all of the capital accounting procedures that we discussed in Chapters 2 (Cost When Sold) and 4 (Allocation Discipline).

The third disposition difference has to do with your date of acquisition. If you acquired the asset before October 22, 1986, you could have taken greater writeoffs than your actual investment. You could have done this because, prior to this date, the at-risk rules (Form 6198) and passive loss rules (Form 8582) were not in full force and effect then. When you've written off more than your actual investment, you have a counterbalancing *write on* — called "phantom income" — when you dispose of that investment. For example, you put up $10,000 and wrote off $16,582. When you dispose of your interest, you have a phantom capital gain of $6,852! You cannot have a conduit interest and write off more than the actual mount of your investment at risk.

If you acquired the asset after October 22, 1986, in all likelihood you would be saddled with an accumulation of unused and aggregated loss carryovers. If you have such carryovers, you have to separate and allocate them "entity by entity." You can use the allocated unused losses to offset any remaining positive amount of your capital account in the entity. When you do so, you may find that your net asset value is zero, negative, or nearly so.

To be quite blunt about it, most conduit interests are difficult to sell, exchange, or terminate. The exceptions are prorata interests in real estate, tangible equipment, consumer inventory, accounts receivable, and portfolio assets (if any). If these entity assets are nonexistent or overencumbered with debt, your best bet is to try to dispose of your interest any way you can for $1 or so. If you cannot do this, you might abandon your interest after giving due notice to the entity manager. In one way or another, you want to clear your tax accounting records.

8

RENTAL REAL ESTATE

Investment Real Estate Generates Gross Income In Two Forms: Rents And Royalties. Rental Property Benefits From A Depreciation Allowance, Whereas Royalty Property Benefits From A Depletion Allowance. In Addition, Both Properties Are Allowed To Deduct From Gross Income All Necessary Operating Expenses For the Year, Provided The Property Is Not Personally Used: Section 212. If Owner Managed And The Total Expenses Produce A Net Loss, A Special $25,000 Loss Rule Applies: Section 469(i). Any Unallowed Current Losses May Be Carried Forward Yearly And ADDED — Allocably — To The Cost Basis Of Each Property When Sold.

As always, another investment option is rental (and royalty) real estate. Said investment involves land, its natural resources, and improvements thereto. Although land, etc. is often the focus of conduit entities, it is also an asset frequently acquired by individual investors. The advantage of real estate to individual investors is that they can manage their own property . . . without a "middleman." When they do so, they partake directly in the tax benefits therefrom.

Investment real estate has four noteworthy attributes. One: It produces — or can produce — significant amounts of current income. Two: It has the potential for appreciation when sold. Three: It provides a modest tax sheltering of its income, during its holding period. Four: It can be owned by one investor (and his spouse), or by two or more investors (and their spouses) without being a formalized entity.

Once the investment realty is legally owned and titled, income is generated by the *use* of the property by persons or entities **other than** the legal owner(s). We want to stress the importance of this nonowner use. Otherwise, except for de minimis personal use, the investment tax benefits fail.

Rental/royalty property may be used for residential, commercial, industrial, extractive, farming, fishing, sports, or other income-producing purposes. In whatever form the land is used, there are certain tax principles which apply. These principles differ markedly from those discussed in the preceding chapters on sterile assets, portfolio assets, and conduit assets.

For example, individually-owned rental realty can — subject to certain conditions — use up to $25,000 of losses annually to offset other positive sources of income of investors. No other investment form can match this one particular tax feature. There are also other differing tax features.

Rents vs. Royalties

Investment real estate can generate either rental income or royalty income. Although, conceivably, it could generate both types of income simultaneously, in practice this seldom happens. Rental property is used for residential shelter and the housing of nonresidential activities, whereas royalty property is used for the extraction of its natural resources. Consequently, the two income forms are quite different.

Rental property generates "rents" for the owner(s) thereof. The amount of rent is based on use of the property per *unit of time*. The unit of time may be per week, per month, or per year. It may also be for a period of several years. During the contracted-use period, the realty owner does not participate in the income of the user (tenant) of the realty. As a result, the amount of rental income tends to be uniform during the rental-use period.

In contrast, royalty property generates "royalties" for the owner(s) thereof. The amount of royalty is based on use of the property per *unit of production*. The unit of production may be per pound, per barrel, per bushel, per ton, per 1000 cubic feet, per acre, or other suitable measure of productivity. Units of productivity are used because the tenant is interested in the property only for the extraction and sale of its natural resources. These resources may be oil, gas, geothermal energy, sand, gravel, gemstones, marble, granite, gold, timber, coal, fruits, nuts, grains, vegetables, fish, game, or whatever. Depending on the amount of resource extracted and sold, there is a royalty to be paid. As a consequence, the amount of royalty income tends to be nonuniform during the royalty-use period.

To derive tax benefits from investment realty, there must be a clear landlord-tenant relationship between the owner(s) and user(s). That is, there must be some contractual form (preferably a written document) spelling out the income amounts and conditions for using the property. Word-of-mouth and handshake arrangements are always tax suspect. Particularly so, if you, members of your family, or close business associates use the property in any substantial way.

Therefore, as an investor, if you are going to own real estate for income-production purposes, you should familiarize yourself with those contractual documents customarily used. Although you could prepare an acceptable written document yourself, it is wise to first check with others who own property similar to yours. Or, you might want to obtain standard legal forms or consult with a real estate attorney. The point that we are trying to make is that you must have some arms-length document defining the terms between yourself and your tenant(s). Otherwise, the IRS will assert personal-use property and deny you all investment-use benefits.

Depreciation vs. Depletion

Once the distinction between rental property and royalty property is clear, there are two tax benefits which immediately accrue. The income from rental property can be offset, to some extent, by a *depreciation* allowance. Similarly, the income from royalty property can be offset, somewhat, by a *depletion* allowance. Both of these income-offset allowances are Congressionally sanctioned in the Federal tax code. The depreciation allowance is set forth in Sections 167 and 168, whereas the depletion allowance is set forth in Sections 611 through 613A.

As defined in Section 167(a), depreciation is an allowable deduction against income for—

> *the exhaustion, wear and tear (including a reasonable allowance for obsolescence) . . . of property held for the production of income.*

For rental real estate, there are only two classes of depreciable assets: residential and nonresidential. The depreciable portions are the building(s), structure(s), and improvements to land. Land in and of itself does not depreciate. Nonland residential property can be depreciated over 27.5 years, whereas nonresidential property can be depreciated over 31.5 years [Sec. 168(c)(1)].

When depreciating rental real estate, only the straight-line method of depreciation can be used [Sec. 168(b)(3)]. Thus, if you are an owner of residential or nonresidential property whose buildings, structures, and improvements cost $300,000, you could write off approximately $10,000 per year against the income from that property. Against a $30,000 annual gross income, for example, a $10,000 depreciation writeoff is indeed a worthwhile tax benefit.

In contrast, depletion is an allowance for the extraction and exhaustion of natural resources from within, on, or adjacent to land in its pristine state. As with depreciation, land itself is not depletable (for tax purposes). Yes, we know that land can erode, slide away, or be carted away, but this is not what the depletion allowance is for. Taxwise, land and its natural resources can be cost separated. The depletion allowance applies only to the separable natural resources.

The tax law on point is Section 611(a), which reads in part—

In the case of mines, oil and gas, wells, other natural deposits, and timber, there shall be allowed as a deduction in computing taxable income a reasonable allowance for depletion . . . according to the peculiar conditions in each case.

There are two kinds of depletion allowances, namely: cost depletion and percentage depletion. Cost depletion is used where the commercial extent of the natural resource can be established with certainty. Standing timber is a good example. The age, quality, height, and circumferences of all standing trees can be physically measured and cost appraised. Cost depletion implies the expectation of full removal of the commercial resource. The remaining land is for rejuvenation purposes.

Percentage depletion is used where the true extent of the natural resource cannot be established with commercial certainty. Estimates, guesses, and risks have to be assumed. Because of these costing uncertainties, a specified percentage of the gross income derived from extracting the resource is allowed as a deduction.

Percentage depletion is most commonly used in mining, drilling, quarrying, and other resource separative techniques.

The percentage depletion allowances are set forth in Sections 613 and 613A of the tax code. They range from a high of 22% to a low of 5% of the gross income of the resource extracted. In general, the more difficult and uncertain the extraction, the higher the depletion allowance. The extraction of sand, gravel, shale, peat, clay, and brine, for example, is allowed only a 5% depletion offset [Sec. 613(b)(6)].

Other Allowable Expenses

For investment real estate which is individually owned (or co-owned), Section 212 of the Internal Revenue Code is very clear. It allows for the deduction against gross income of other expenses than depreciation and depletion. This tax code section reads in full below.

Sec. 212 - Expenses for production of income

In the case of an individual, there shall be allowed all of the ordinary and necessary expenses paid or incurred during the taxable year—

(1) for the production or collection of income;
(2) for the management, conservation, or maintenance of property held for the production of income; or
(3) in connection with the determination, collection, or refund of any tax.

So, what are the "other" allowable expenses?

For starters, they include such expenses as property taxes (including severance taxes), mortgage interest, other interest paid (relating to the property or its maintenance), insurance (casualty and liability), utilities (paid for by landlord for tenant), repairs and maintenance to the property . . . and a host of other property-related expenditures.

In summary form, we list in Figure 8.1 all of the eligible expenditures which are deductible for income property. They apply whether rental or royalty property is involved. There are certain expenditures, however, to which we want especially to call your attention.

RENTAL INCOME		ROYALTY INCOME		
EXPENSES: EACH PROPERTY ➤		A	B	C
1.	Advertising			
2.	Auto & travel			
3.	Cleaning & maintenance			
4.	Commissions			
5.	Insurance			
6.	Legal & professional fees			
7.	Mortgage interest			
8.	Other interest			
9.	Repairs			
10.	Supplies			
11.	Taxes			
12.	Utilities			
13.	Wages & salaries			
14.	Other (specify)	▨	▨	▨
	● Dues & pubs			
	● Licenses & permits			
	● Pool & gardening			
	● Hardware & misc.			
	● Small appliances			
DEPRECIATION ALLOWANCE		DEPLETION ALLOWANCE		

Fig. 8.1 - Allowable Expenses Against Rental / Royalty Income

Do note in Figure 8.1 the expense item designated as: *Auto and travel.* Please don't get carried away on this one. It's a tax trap. Your auto and travel expenses are limited strictly to the managing and maintenance of the property that you currently own. Travel expenses do not apply to property which you hope to own. Nor do they apply to expenses for attending seminars or conventions, whether real estate or other type of investments. Section 274(h)(7) says very specifically—

> *No deduction shall be allowed under section 212 for expenses allocable to a convention, seminar, or similar meeting.*

The term "auto" relates to local mileage (at approximately 26¢ per mile) to and from your property, and to and from the suppliers of tools, equipment, and materials for repairs and maintenance of your property. The term "travel" means away overnight *at* your property, should it be located at more than a normal day's commute drive. Any travel to out-of-state property should be limited to once a year, or twice, at most. And then only for good reason. Could you not have handled the matter by phone or mail?

Caution With Hirees

There's still another tax trap in Figure 8.1. It encompasses several of the items listed: commissions, cleaning and maintenance, legal and professional fees, repairs, and wages and salaries. These are those expenses that you pay, or may pay, to various persons (hirees) for services rendered in connection with your property.

All real estate requires the attention and services of persons other than yourself. If the services are performed on a regular and continuing basis, you may trip yourself into the role of becoming an *employer* of your hirees. Should this happen, you become engulfed in a whole new arena: the **employer tax world**.

We don't want to get into employer tax matters. Nor should you. It is complicated and full of quarterly tax returns, wage and tax statements, social security taxes (which you pay), health insurance payments, and employer penalties. Then, when you are through tangling with the IRS on these matters, state tax employment agencies enter the scene to harass you further.

Our advice is: As a property owner, stay away from employer tax matters. Stick to your role as an investor. Don't become an employer. You can do this by making sure that the persons you hire are either in business for themselves or are independent contractors. These are persons or entities who perform a service on a job contract basis. When they do so, they submit to you a billing on an invoice, using their business letterhead. For each service payment, you need a separate invoice. Each invoice becomes your documentary evidence that a nonemployee relationship exists.

Schedule E (1040) Part I

As owner of investment real estate, there is one particular tax form that you should become well familiar with (if you are not already so). This is Schedule E (Form 1040), Part I: **Income or Loss From Rentals and Royalties**. The overall Schedule E itself is titled: Supplemental Income and Loss. Parts II, III, and IV thereof address those conduit entities which we covered previously in Chapter 7.

So long as you hold rental/royalty property for investment purposes, you must complete Schedule E, Part I each year. Therefore, for familiarization purposes, we present in Figure 8.2 an edited and abbreviated version of Part I, Schedule E. This schedule attaches directly to your regular Form 1040.

There are approximately 30 line entries on the official version of Schedule E. We have purposely omitted the official line numbers in Figure 8.2 so that you can grasp better the functional aspects of the form, rather than its line entry details. Please take a moment now to glance at Figure 8.2.

As you should immediately note, each Schedule E is structured to accommodate three properties only. If you own more than three properties, you must use continuation Schedule E's and mark them, respectively, as E-1, E-2, E-3, and so on. As with all continuation schedules, you bring the grand totals forward to the very last Schedule E that you use. Otherwise, you foul up the IRS's computer.

You should also note in Figure 8.2 that it requires that each property be incomed, expensed, and depreciated/depleted entirely separately from all others. Except for the grand totals, you cannot aggregate the income and expenses of your properties. The reason for this is that each property can be disposed of separately. When disposition of a property occurs, you have to show its own capital gain/loss computation on an entirely separate form, namely: Form 4797 (Sales of Business Property).

Also note in Figure 8.2 the head caution which reads—

Your rental loss may be limited. See Instructions.

Schedule E (Form 1040)	SUPPLEMENTAL INCOME AND LOSS			Year

Your Name: **Soc.Sec.No.**

Part I   **Income or Loss From Rentals and Royalties**

Caution: Your rental loss may be limited. See instructions.

Kind and location each property				yes	no
A	Question I ● Personal Use?	A B C			
B	Question II ● Participation?	A B C			
C					

● Rents ● Royalties	Properties			Totals
	A	**B**	**C**	
Gross Income ➤				
Expenses				
➤				
➤				
➤				
See Fig. 8.1 ➤				
➤				
➤				
➤				
Subtotal Expenses ➤				
Depreciation / Depletion				
Total Expenses ➤				
NET INCOME OR LOSS (subtract total expenses from gross income)				
Allowable Loss (from Form 8582)	< >	< >	< >	
Add net incomes from all properties ➤				
Add allowable losses from all properties ➤			< >	
AGGREGATE NET INCOME OR LOSS ➤				

Fig. 8.2 - Edited/Abbreviated Version of Schedule E (Part I)

The instructions regarding net losses focus on Form 6198 (At-Risk Limitations) and Form 8582 (Passive Activity Loss Limitations).

We touched on these two loss-limitation forms in the preceding chapter. So there is no need for our rehashing them here.

The deductible expense items in Figure 8.2 are identical to those detailed in Figure 8.1. When you total the expenses and deductions for each property, and the result is a net loss, the small print instructions (on Schedule E) remind you again to check the loss limitation Forms 6198 and 8582.

Two "Yes"-"No" Questions

The head portion of each Schedule E, Part I, contains two check-box questions. You must answer each question "Yes" or "No." Furthermore, you must answer each question separately for each property. We tried to indicate this separate property check-boxing in Figure 8.2.

Question I reads in full as—

For each rental property listed on line 1, did you or your family use it for personal purposes for more than the greater of 14 days or 10% of the total days rented at fair rental value during the tax year.   ☐ *Yes*   ☐ *No*

If you answer "No" to this question, you can deduct all of your expenses, subject only to the loss limitation rules.

If you answer "Yes" to Question I and rented the unit out for less than 15 days, you cannot deduct any expenses on Schedule E. The property is treated as personal-use property subject to limited deductions for mortgage interest and property taxes on Schedule A: Itemized Personal Deductions.

If you answer "Yes" to Question I and rented the property for 15 days or more, you have to prorate all expenses (including depreciation) in proportion to the number of days actually rented for the year. For example, if you rented the property for 100 days, the allowable fraction of each expense item on Schedule E is 100/365 or 0.273. The net effect is that you cannot deduct allocable expenses that exceed your gross rental income for the year. Thereafter, any unallowed mortgage interest and property taxes may be claimed on Schedule A (1040). Any other unallowable rental expenses may be carried forward on Schedule E for the subsequent year.

Question II reads in full as—

*For each **rental real estate property** listed on line 1, did you actively participate in its operation during the tax year?*

☐ *Yes*   ☐ *No*

If you answer "No" to this question, you are subject to all of the loss limitation rules involving Forms 6198 and 8582. In general, these rules limit your aggregate net losses from all properties to the aggregate net incomes from all nonloss properties. Any unallowable losses are carried forward — allocably (property by property) — to the subsequent year.

If you answer "Yes" to Question II, you may be eligible to aggregate your net losses from all properties up to $25,000 and write these losses off against your other sources of positive income. There is a special rule on this, which we present below.

The $25,000 Loss Rule

The rules on passive activity loss limits are set forth in Section 469 of the tax code. This section consists of approximately 3,250 words of tax law. Among its many features and restrictions against loss writeoffs, it defines a "passive activity" as any activity — including rental real estate — in which the taxpayer does not materially participate (with his personal services). As we initially informed you in Chapter 1: Investor Defined, this is the very characteristic which defines an investment . . . and avoids the Social Security/Medicare tax.

But in passing Section 469 in October 1986, Congress wanted to carve out an exception for small investors who owner-manage their rental real estate. Thereupon, **Section 469(i)** was prescribed. This subsection is titled: **$25,000 Offset for rental real estate activities**. This is strictly a "special allowance" loss feature.

The gist of Section 469(i) is that for owner-managed investment realty, an aggregate of $25,000 of net losses (from all properties) may be allowable. This maximum amount is allowable annually for a married couple filing jointly.

There is one proviso in Section 469(i). The $25,000 offset applies only to those Form 1040 filers whose modified adjusted gross income does not exceed $100,000. There is total phase-out of this offset when the modified AGI exceeds $150,000. These amounts are cut in half for married persons filing separately.

The key to allowability of the $25,000 offset is the statutory term: *active participation*. This term is defined in the official instructions to Schedule E (Part I) as—

The active participation requirement can be met without regular, continuous, and substantial involvement in operations. But you must have participated in making management decisions or arranging for others to provide services (such as repairs), in a significant and bona fide sense. Management decisions that are relevant in this context include approving new tenants, deciding on rental terms, approving capital or repair expenditures, and other similar decisions.

Once you check "Yes" to the active participation question on Schedule E, and you have an aggregate net loss from your rental properties, Part II of Form 8582 (Passive Activity Loss Limitations) comes into play. This part is titled: *Computation of the Special Allowance for Rental Real Estate With Active Participation*. The computational mechanics involved are set forth in Figure 8.3.

Form 8582	Passive Activity Loss Limitations				Year
Part II	**Rental Real Estate With Active Participation**				
1	Enter total pertinent losses from Schedule E				$
2	Enter $150,000		✱	$	
3	Enter modified AGI	but not less than zero	$		
4	Subtract 3 from 2	but not less than zero	$		
5	Multiply Line 4 by 50%	Do not enter more than $25,000		✱	$
6	Enter the SMALLER of Line 1 or Line 5				$
Allocate Line 6 proportionately to each property in Line 1					
	✱ See instructions for married filing separately				

Fig. 8.3 - Computation of Allowable Losses for Rental Real Estate

The allowable loss computation is relatively easy to follow. The only catch is the term "modified" adjusted gross income. This is your ordinary AGI (very last line on page 1 of Form 1040) **without inclusion** of any passive activity income or loss otherwise entered on Form 8582. The point being made in Figure 8.3 is that the allowable special loss may indeed be less than $25,000. It could even be zero.

Loss Carryover Allocations

As Figure 8.3 implies, not all of your aggregate losses from rental real estate may be allowed. For any given year, some or all may be unallowable. Consequently, the logical question arises: What happens to your unallowable losses? Are they lost forever?

No, your unallowable losses are not totally lost. They are "suspended."

Section 469(b) prescribes that any properly computed unallowable loss may be carried forward to the next succeeding taxable year. It may be carried forward year after year until the investment asset is disposed of in its entirety [Sec. 469(g)]. When the property is sold (or exchanged), its cumulative unallowed losses add to its tax basis for determining capital gain or capital loss.

The catch is that if you have more than one piece of rental property, your aggregate unallowed losses must be allocated to each property separately. This is Chapter 5: Allocation Discipline, revisited.

For example, suppose you have three rental properties: A, B, and C. Also suppose that, by properly using Form 8582 (which includes a line entry for "prior year unallowed losses"), your aggregate three-property cumulative losses are $35,000. You sell property B. What is your carryover loss adjustment to basis in that property when it is sold?

It is NOT $35,000. It is some other figure (probably much lower) depending on the unallowed losses allocable to properties A and C. That is, the $35,000 would have to have been cumulatively allocated between properties A, B, and C as you went along, year by year. Chances are, your tax man or accountant would have done this for you automatically. If not, the instructions to Form 8582 provide worksheets for figuring it out yourself.

The point that we're making, we believe, is rather obvious. If — for whatever reason — all of your bona fide rental losses cannot be used in a given tax year, you have a loss carryover accounting system to maintain. Set up any system that properly reflects the allocable losses to each property. You can do this on the back of Form 8582, which is blank, and transfer each property's cumulative loss allocation to that property's unrecovered basis. Thus, each property's unused allocable loss becomes an **addition** to its "cost or other basis" when disposed of in a fully taxable transaction.

The tax law on point does not specifically say: "add to cost basis." In paraphrased form, Sec. 469(g)(1) says—

If during the taxable year a taxpayer disposes of his entire interest in any passive activity . . . any loss from such activity [which has not been previously allowed as a deduction] . . . shall be allowable as a deduction . . . against any gain recognized on the disposition.

In other words, your suspended losses become a *deduction* against any dispositional gain. Since this reduces gain, it gives the same result as addition to cost basis.

Here's a simple example of how suspended losses are used when property is sold. Consider that you bought a piece of rental realty for $160,000. The cumulative depreciation allowable was $50,000; the cumulative suspended losses (previously disallowed) were $35,000. The property sells for $200,000 (after selling expenses). What is the net gain?

Answer:

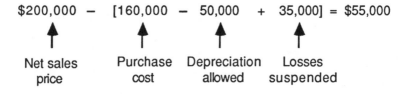

$$\$200,000 - [160,000 - 50,000 + 35,000] = \$55,000$$

| Net sales price | Purchase cost | Depreciation allowed | Losses suspended |

As an investor, you probably do not intend to keep your rental properties forever. As the opportunity arises, you'd probably sell (or exchange) them one at a time. When you do, your cumulative passive loss carryovers will come in handy. They will definitely provide a tax benefit that you may not have considered before. In our example above, without the suspended losses the gain would have been $90,000 (55,00 + 35,000) instead of the $55,000 shown. The less gain, the less tax.

9

SPECIAL SITUATIONS

A Different Tax World Awaits Sophisticated Investors. Because Their Activities Are More Complex, Special Tax Rules — And Tax Forms — Come Into Play. Stock Cloning Requires Stringent Reallocation Of Cost; Contracts And Straddles Require Form 6781; Farm Rentals (Sharecropping) Require Form 4835; Casualties And Thefts Require Form 4684. Investing In Franchises And Trademarks Requires A Knowledge Of Section 1253. Disposition Of "Section 1231 Property" Enjoys Capital Gain, Ordinary Loss Treatment. Dispositions Of "Recapture Property," Involuntary Conversions, And Other Transactions Are Reported On Form 4797.

There is a host of investment options other than those discussed in the preceding chapters. There are some rather complicated and not run-of-the-mill activities. They involve new terminology, stringent allocation accounting, new sections of the tax code, and — of course — new tax forms. These activities comprise an assortment of assets, spinoffs, and arrangements that are of more interest to sophisticated investors than to ordinary investors.

A sophisticated investor is one who does not shun complexity in his capital transactions. Indeed, complexity itself is sometimes the rewarding investment challenge. A sophisticated investor is also one who is not emotionally destroyed by his losses. Losses — sometimes large losses — are accepted as part of the ups and downs of investment cycles. Although worldly wise and risk hardened, sophisticated investors can overlook important tax rules.

In this chapter, therefore, we want to pull together some of the more uncommon investment activities, and point out the tax features involved. Among such activities are stock cloning (and basis reallocation), contracts and straddles, rental of farm land (and sale), Section 1231 property, Section 1245 property, franchises and trademarks, casualties and thefts, involuntary conversions, and catchall Form 4797. In the full investment world of gains and losses, things *can get* quite complicated. This is the very point we try to make in our lead-off illustration below.

Stock Cloning Illustration

You are an avid portfolio investor who holds on for a long time. No frequent telephone switching for you. You are an environmentally sensitive person who has latched onto an up-to-date coal mining company responsive to "clean air" objectives worldwide. You paid $12,000 for 100 shares of common stock in the New World Coal Company. Your NWC stock is listed on the One-World Stock Exchange as a sure winner for growth.

In addition to mining the coal in the U.S. and abroad, the company also builds and operates coking plants, gasification plants, liquefaction plants, transport colliers, air scrubbers, electrical transmission lines, etc. In the process of its growth, the company issues to existing investors all sorts of stock options, stock rights, stock warrants, stock splits, preferred stock, debentures, and so on. This is called "stock cloning." Stock cloning is a bonus benefit when corporate growth is successful.

Initially, you paid $120 per share for the NWC common stock ($12,000 ÷ 100 shares). Several years later, you receive a nontaxable distribution in the form of 35 shares of preferred stock. As a result of its growth, the company reorganized and made these distributions to you at no cost.

Several years later, again you were offered stock rights to buy 50 shares of common. You exercised 25 of your stock rights and bought at the option price of $125 per share. You bought the other 25 rights (at $15 per share) to exercise in the future.

As time goes on, you are offered still more stock clones. But it begins to dawn on you that, someday, you might sell your initial stock and its clones. When you do, you sense that there may be severe reallocation-of-cost problems, so you buy no more clones.

Years pass and you decide to sell. You call your worldwide stock broker. He gives you the latest market quotation as follows:

Common stock	$150 per share
Preferred stock	80 per share
Stock rights	15 per share

You glance at Schedule D: Capital Gains and Losses, and you read aloud to yourself the heading at Column (e). It says: *Cost or other basis (see instructions)*. Now, we ask you—

What is **your** cost basis in the common stock? The preferred stock? The stock rights?

Did you keep track chronologically of the shares you acquired and the money you paid? Are you aware that you have to *completely reallocate* your cost basis for each of the three kinds of stock that you now hold? Let's make things simple and assume that you never automatically reinvested your dividends. You took them in cash and paid the dividends tax each year.

Repeating the above: What is your cost basis in the common stock? The preferred stock? The stock rights?

We'll run through the answer so that you get the "flavor" of the reallocation effort required.

Two Distinct Phases

There are two distinct phases for arriving at the final answers. *Phase I*: Reallocation of basis of the old stock (100 shares @ $120 per share) for the nontaxable distribution. Since you were not taxed on this distribution, the preferred stock and stock rights share proportionately in your initial investment. *Phase II*: Readjustment of basis for additional purchases.

Phase I — **Reallocation of Basis**

Initial basis old stock (100 shares @ $120)	$12,000
Market value old stock (100 shares @ $150)	15,000
Market value preferred stock (35 shares @ $80)	2,800
Market value stock rights (50 shares @ $15)	750
Total market value: ex-distribution	$18,500

Old stock portion of total market value	
$15,000 ÷ 18,500	0.8082
Preferred stock portion of total market value	
$ 2,800 ÷ 18,500	0.1513
Stock rights portion of total market value	
$ 750 ÷ 18,500	0.0405
	1.0000

Revised basis old stock	
0.8082 x $12,000	$ 9,698
Initial basis preferred stock	
0.1513 x $12,000	1,816
Initial basis stock rights	
0.0405 x $12,000	486
	$12,000

Phase II — Readjustment of Basis

Revised basis common stock (100 shares)	$ 9,698
Additional common stock purchased	
25 shares @ $125 per share	3,125
	$12,823

Initial basis stock rights (50 shares)	486
Actual stock rights purchased	
25 shares @ $15 per share	375
Basis of 25 shares of stock rights	861

(Note: the exercise of 25 rights reduced the possessory rights from 50 to 25.)

Final Answers:

125 shares common for	$12,823 = $102.58 per share
35 shares preferred for	1,816 = 51.86 per share
25 stock rights for	861 = 34.44 per share

If you sold at the broker quotations above, you would derive capital gain from the common stock and from the preferred stock. You would suffer a capital loss by selling the stock rights. Your cost basis is $34.44 per share, whereas they would sell for only $15 per share. However, this loss could be used — on Schedule D — to offset your common/preferred stock gains, dollar for dollar.

Contracts & Straddles

In the go-go world of sophisticated investing, there is a *paper-on-paper* class of portfolio activity known as "contracts and straddles." Corporate debt and equity, as well as rights to commodity assets, are identified by ownership paper stating the number of shares or number of units owned. Masking this ownership paper is another form of paper characterized as contracts, options, straddles, and futures. The acquirer of masking paper (paper-on-paper) never intends to acquire the underlying ownership security to which it attaches.

Masking (nonownership) paper is tax recognized as a capital asset. This is because of its unique self-enforcing feature. Namely, an investor loses his total investment if he does not settle his outstanding contracts, or offset his unexpired straddles in a timely manner. All forms of contracts and straddles are highly sophisticated. In the tax code, they are referred to as **Section 1256 Contracts** (2,500 words) and **Section 1092 Straddles** (3,300 words). The tax rules are too complex for other than our passing comment here.

A Section 1256 contract is any (1) regulated futures contract, (2) foreign currency contract, (3) nonequity option, or (4) dealer equity option. The tax reporting on these items is done in terms of: (a) *realized* profits or loses, (b) **unrealized** profits or losses, and (c) aggregate profits or losses. Amounts "realized" are those occurring when a contract is settled before its expiration date. Amounts "unrealized" are those determined on open contracts under *marked-to-market* rules (market value) as of December 31 of each taxable year. Aggregate amounts are the net netting of realized and unrealized profit and losses. It is the aggregate amount — either profit or loss — that is reported on one's tax return. A separate aggregate entry is made for each brokerage account: NOT each contract. This differs from the separate reporting of each sale or exchange of ownership paper.

A Section 1092 straddle is an "offsetting position" to alter the tax character of one's primary holdings or Section 1256 contracts. Assets used for straddle purposes are commodity items (such as gold or silver) or debt instruments (such as Treasury notes or municipal bonds). The IRS presumption is that a straddle is undertaken for tax reasons rather than for profit reasons. Consequently, any loss sustained by a straddle or series of straddles is limited to one's unrealized (unexercised) gains in related straddles.

A special tax form is used to report contracts and straddles. It is **Form 6781**: Gains and Losses From Section 1256 Contracts and Straddles. The form comprises three parts, namely:

Part I   — Section 1256 Contracts Marked to Market
Part II   — Gains and Losses From Straddles
• Sec. A   — Losses From Straddles
• Sec. B   — Gains From Straddles
Part III   — Unrealized Gains From Positions Held on Last
                Day of Tax Year

Instructions on Form 6781 direct you to make short-term or long-term entries on Schedule D (1040) as appropriate.

Rental of Farm Land

A situation that develops from time to time is that a taxpayer — it could be you — inherits vast acreage of farmland from his parental lineage. The inheritee has no intention of farming the land himself. So he sharecrops it out. That is, he rents it to others who are more farming disposed than himself. This includes renting a farm house (to the sharecropper and his family), farm equipment (tractors, combines, cultivators), irrigation system (well, pump, piping), and other structures (fencing, barns, silos).

When you rent farmland and actively participate in its overall management, it takes on the same tax character as investment realty discussed in Chapter 8: Rental Real Estate. However, there are differences in the nature of the income and in the nature of the expenses allowed.

A sharecropper does not pay rent money in the ordinary sense. He "pays" a share of the livestock, grain, and other crops that he produces. The percentage of crop sharing is set forth in a share-cropping agreement. It's almost like a general partnership: the sharecropper and his family provide all of the labor; the farm owner provides the land, the equipment, and pays virtually all operating expenses. In some cases, the cost of seed, feed, fertilizer, and chemicals is shared. The essential elements of a sharecropping agreement (for tax purposes) is presented in Figure 9.1. It is analogous to a rental/royalty agreement. It must be in writing.

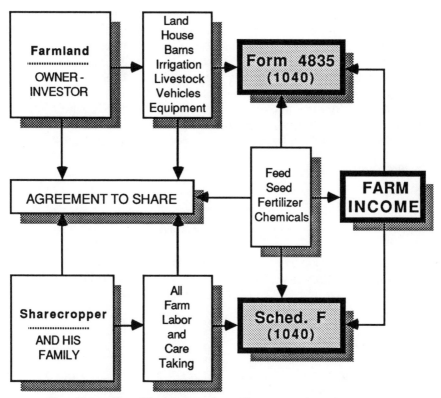

Fig. 9.1 - Tax Elements of a Sharecropping Agreement

The owner's income from sharecropping his farm land is comprised of the following forms:

1. Owner's share of livestock, grain, and crop sales (including poultry, produce, fruit, nuts, fish, etc.).
2. Patronage dividends from farm cooperatives.
3. Department of Agriculture program payments.
4. Crop pledges against Commodity Credit Corporation loans.
5. Crop insurance proceeds and disaster payments.
6. Gasoline and fuel tax credits and refunds.

The sum of these items comprises the *gross farm rents* for the taxable year. Not being the actual farmer of the land, the owner pays no social security tax on this income.

Against the farm gross rents, the owner writes off all of the ordinary and necessary farm operating expenses. This includes a depreciation allowance for all buildings, improvements, and equipment. In addition, the owner can claim soil and water conservation expenses — called "Section 175" expenses.

All farmland rents and expenses are reported on **Form 4835**: Farm Rental Income and Expenses. It is attached to one's annual return (Form 1040) after certain inclusions on Schedule E (1040). If the "bottom line" on Form 4835 is a net loss for the year—

You MUST check the box that describes your investment in this activity:
☐ *All investment is at risk*
☐ *Some investment is not at risk*

If you actively participated in the farm rental management, and all your ownership investment is at risk, you can deduct your net loss to the extent of $25,000 when combined with all other rental/royalty real estate (if any).

Section 1231 Property

There is a special class of property known to sophisticated investors, but not so well known to ordinary investors. It is called "Section 1231 property." The "1231" is the leadoff section of the tax code where special rules apply for determining capital gains and losses.

Section 1231 carries the official heading: **Property used in the trade or business and involuntary conversions**. Actually, an investor himself does not have to be in a trade or business to get the special tax benefits of Section 1231. So long as he owns the property and rents or leases it to someone or some entity who uses the property in a trade or business, the owner/investor gets the 1231 treatment. The best examples of this are investments in limited partnerships, S corporations, business trusts, rental/royalty realty, farm land rental, equipment rentals, breeding stock, and the like.

In essence, Section 1231 property is any capital asset held for more than one year "in connection with" a trade or business or a transaction entered into for profit. It includes investment real estate, tangible property such as machinery and equipment, timber, coal, iron ore, cattle and horses, livestock (other than poultry), unharvested crop, and other depreciable/depletable assets.

Regarding the property above, what does Section 1231 say?

In paraphrased form, Section 1231(a)(1),(2) says that—

(1) If the section 1231 gains exceed the section 1231 losses, the net gain shall be treated as long-term capital gain.

(2) If the section 1231 losses exceed the section 1231 gains, the net loss shall be treated as an ordinary loss: **not** a capital loss.

This is called the "capital gain-ordinary loss" rule.

What is so special about this rule?

It is special because if the Section 1231 transactions result in a net loss, there is no applicable loss limitation as in the case of passive losses and capital losses. That is, the Section 1231 losses can be used to offset other positive sources of income without limit.

Now you know why Section 1231 is a valuable investment tool for informed taxpayers.

Section 1245 Property

Now, let's tell you about another category that could turn out to be a tax trap for the unsophisticated. This is "Section 1245" property. Such property consists primarily of depreciable-type assets other than residential-type buildings and their structural components. The "1245" focuses on vehicles, machinery, equipment, storage vessels, transportation facilities, and the like. It targets those tangible assets which benefit from favorable tax rules during their holding period.

Section 1245 is titled: **Gain from disposition of certain depreciable property**. Take care to note the qualifying word "certain." The *certain* is spelled out in Section 1245(a)(3) which defines Section 1245 property as—

Any property which is or has been property of a character subject to allowance for depreciation provided in section 167 . . . and is either—

(A) personal property [as contrasted to real property],

(B) other property (not including a building or its structural components) . . .

> *(i) used as an integral part of manufacturing, production, or extraction . . .,*
> *(C) so much of any real property* [as adjusted] *for amortization under sections 169* [pollution control facilities], *179* [election to expense certain assets] *. . .,*
> *(D) a single purpose agricultural or horticultural structure,*
> *(E) a storage facility . . . used in connection with the distribution of petroleum or any primary product of petroleum,*
> *(F) any railroad grading or tunnel bore . . . .*

Section 1245 consists of approximately 1,750 words. Its purpose and gist are to *recapture* all depreciation-type benefits previously allowed, when an item is sold, exchanged, or involuntarily converted. "Depreciation-type" benefits include ordinary depreciation, accelerated depreciation, cost recovery allowances, amortization, and expense elections (in lieu of depreciation).

If Section 1245 property is sold at a gain (over its adjusted basis), all gain is ordinary gain to the extent of all prior depreciation "allowed or allowable." If sold at a price greater than its initial acquisition cost, the amount of gain above initial cost is capital gain. If sold at a price less than its adjusted basis, there is no recapture. The loss may be ordinary, capital, or nonrecognized, depending on the use of the property at the time of its sale.

Section 1245 states the above in complex wordage. We prefer to portray the end result in diagrammatic form. This is done in Figure 9.2 for different sale situations.

In essence, the tax trap aspects of Section 1245 is that it recaptures all prior special benefits which were expensed. This is called *recapture gain* in contrast to capital gain. Recapture gain is often a surprise to unwary investors.

Other "Recapture" Property

Section 1245 inaugurates a tax benefit recall process which is applicable to other property items. Foremost in this regard is Section 1231 property itself. Section 1231(c) — which we did not tell you about previously — recaptures all prior net 1231 losses within a 5-year period. The effect is that any current-year capital gain from Section 1231 property is treated as *ordinary gain*, to the

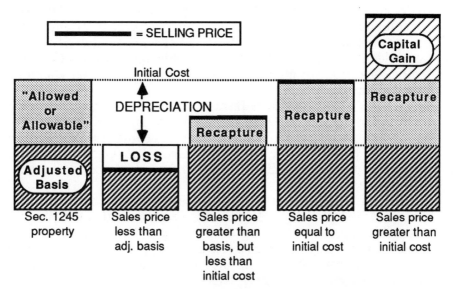

Fig. 9.2 - Concept of Depreciation Recapture for Nonrealty

extent of any nonrecaptured 1231 losses. Ordinary gain adds to other sources of positive income without any offsetting deductions.

Let's use a numerical example. In 1987, you incurred a 1231 net loss of $5,000, and in 1989 you incurred a similar loss of $8,000. In 1992 (within five years of the first loss), you had a 1231 net gain of $10,000. What is the tax character of this gain?

The entire $10,000 is ordinary gain. Your cumulative 5-year nonrecaptured losses were $13,000 (5,000 + 8,000). You still have $3,000 (13,000 - 10,000) of nonrecaptured 1231 loss.

If your 1992 Section 1231 net gain had been $15,000 instead of $10,000 you would have $13,000 in ordinary gain and $2,000 in capital gain.

There are also other recapture properties such as—

Sec. 1250 — Depreciable real estate
Sec. 1252 — Certain farm land
Sec. 1254 — Oil, gas, geothermal, and mineral deposits
Sec. 1255 — Government cost-sharing programs

Section 1250 property is residential and nonresidential real estate placed in rental service before 1987. In those prior years, rental realty enjoyed certain accelerated depreciation benefits. The term "accelerated" means that amount which exceeds straight-line depreciation over about 30 years (27.5 years residential; 31.5 years nonresidential). The excess is recapturable upon disposition of the realty. The result is additional capital gain beyond that which an investor normally counts on.

Section 1252 property is farm land for which deductions were allowed for soil and water conservation expenses, and land clearing expenses, within a 10-year period preceding sale. Section 1252(a)(3) prescribes declining applicable percentages of recovery of those expenses (as ordinary income) for holding periods greater than five years.

Section 1254 property comprises those extractive resources (oil, gas, minerals) for which deductions were allowed for depletion, intangible (dry hole) drilling costs, mine exploration costs, and production development costs. At the time of disposition of these resource interests, the gain, if any, is recharacterized as ordinary income to the extent of all recapturable costs.

Section 1255 property is open space and resource land which, during a 10-year period prior to disposition, received cost-sharing payments from government, which were excludible from gross income. Section 1255(a)(3) prescribes declining applicable percentages of inclusionary income for holding periods greater than 10 years.

In summary, when you dispose of recapture property, you have to show the recapture computation on **Form 4797**: Sales of Business Property. This means keeping accurate tax records of your prior-to-disposition recoverable items. If you fail to keep these records, the IRS treats all gain as recapture gain . . . and taxes you accordingly.

Franchises, Trademarks, Etc.

A tricky area of investor tax law has to do with transfers of franchises, trademarks, and trade names: Section 1253. The transferor (seller?) wants to treat the transaction as a capital asset, whereas the transferee (buyer?) wants to treat it as an amortizable asset. An amortizable asset is one for which the acquisition cost can be written off uniformly (ratably) over some designated period of time, usually 10 years or more. For Section 1253 transactions, tax treatment depends on the character of any *retained interests* in the franchise, etc. transferred.

Section 1253(a) says quite clearly that—

*A transfer of a franchise, trademark, or trade name **shall not** be treated as a sale or exchange of a capital asset if the transferor retains any significant power, right, or continuing interest with respect to the subject matter of the franchise, trademark, or trade name.* [Emphasis added.]

A "significant power, right, or continuing interest" is defined in subsection 1253(b)(2) as—

(A) A right to disapprove any assignment of such interest.
(B) A right to terminate at will.
(C) A right to prescribe the standards of quality of products used or sold, or of services furnished . . .
(D) A right to require that the transferee sell or advertise only the products or services of the transferor.
(E) A right to require that the transferee purchase substantially all supplies and equipment from transferor.
(F) A right to payments contingent on the productivity, use, or disposition of the . . . interest transferred.

In other words, what Sections 1253(a) and (b) mean is that unless a transferee (buyer?) has an absolute right to do what he — **not** the transferor — wants, the transfer is not a bona fide sale. It is more in the nature of a licensing agreement. This is so, even though a substantial principal sum may be paid at the time of the transfer. The result is that all *contingent payments* are ordinary income to the transferor and are expense deductions to the transferee. This is why the terms "seller" and "buyer" were annotated above with a ?-mark.

Where a principal sum (in addition to contingent payments) not exceeding $100,000 is paid, the buyer (transferee) can amortize this amount over 10 years [Sec. 1253(d)(2)]. All principal sums greater than $100,000 shall be capitalized. However, Section 1253(d)(3) allows an election to amortize the excess amount over 25 years.

Notable exceptions to all of the above are professional sports franchises. Section 1253(e) says very succinctly that—

This section shall not apply to the transfer of a franchise to engage in professional football, basketball, baseball, or other professional sport.

Casualties & Thefts

Another tax arena in which investors often find themselves pertains to casualties and thefts. These are situations where the conversion or disposition of assets is not by choice of the investor. Casualties are the destructive forces of fire, storm, shipwreck, earthquake, and other substantial accidents, both natural and man-caused. Theft includes fraud, embezzlement, and misrepresentation.

Let's dramatize the tax point with a realistic example. You are a rare-stamp collector with several authenticated albums valued at $185,000. Your traceable acquisition costs are $65,000. You have your stamp collection insured for $100,000 against theft, counterfeit, fire, flood, etc. You place the stamp albums alongside of you on your car seat. You are on your way to a reputable auction gallery where you intend to sell your collection to the highest bidder.

You are driving across a bridge (over a river). An oncoming truck crosses over the center divider and rams into your vehicle, forcing you against the guard rail. Your car door pops open; your stamp albums flip out, over the rail, into the rushing water below. Your seat belt saves you from major injury. After giving statements to the accident-responding officials, you discover that your stamp albums are missing. What is your tax situation? Assume that you recover the $100,000 insurance.

Believe it or not, you actually have a capital gain! Yes, your gain is $35,000: the $100,000 insurance recovery minus your $65,000 acquisition cost. No, you do not have a $85,000 capital loss (the $185,000 value minus $100,000 insurance). Let us explain.

When computing the tax consequences of a casualty or theft, you must use **Form 4684, Section B**: Casualties and Thefts — Business and Income Producing Property. The computational scheme goes like this:

Step 1 — Cost or other basis of property
Step 2 — Insurance or other reimbursement
Step 3 — (a) If Step 2 is more than Step 1, you have a GAIN. Follow instructions on Form 4684
(b) If Step 1 is more than Step 2, continue to Step 4
Step 4 — Fair market value **before** casualty
Step 5 — Fair market value **after** casualty
Step 6 — **Subtract** Step 5 from Step 4
Step 7 — Enter **smaller** of Step 1 or Step 6

Step 8 — **Subtract** Step 2 (reimbursement) from Step 7. This is your casualty or theft LOSS. Follow instructions on Form 4684.

The message here is clear. No casualty or theft loss is tax recognized until Form 4684 is properly completed. The instructions tell you that you cannot complete the form until you have exhausted all avenues for reimbursement: insurance or otherwise. The reimbursement — whatever amount it is — is your "sales price" for computing gain or loss.

Involuntary Conversions

There is still another category of investment property for which there are special tax rules. This is Section 1033 property: that which is converted to similar or related-in-use property caused by compulsion. The compulsion derives from destruction, seizure, requisition, condemnation, or the threat or imminence thereof. The special tax feature is that there is nonrecognition of gain, if certain conditions for replacement property are met. It is this replacement property aspect that distinguishes involuntary conversions from casualties and thefts.

Eligible Section 1033 property is that which fulfills any bona fide investment objective. It includes (among other items) outdoor advertising displays, livestock destroyed by disease, timber destroyed by drought, assets expropriated by a foreign government, vehicles/equipment destroyed by war, buildings/structures condemned for public use, land blocked off for flood control measures, mandated transactions by government agencies, etc.

The gist of Section 1033 — it consists of approximately 1,800 words — is that the owner/convertee has two options. One: After seeking whatever reimbursement he can get, he can pocket the money and compute his gain or loss similar to casualties and thefts. Or, two: He can take the reimbursement money or property substitute, and acquire replacement property similar in value and nature, in which case he pays no tax. If the replacement property is dissimilar in nature, or is less in value that his reimbursement money, he pays tax on the difference (as capital gain).

The statutory wording on point is contained in Section 1033(a): Its paragraph (1) is: **Conversion into similar property**; paragraph (2) is Conversion into money—

> *If property . . . is compulsorily or involuntarily converted—*
> *(1) Into property similar or related in service or use to the property so converted, **no gain shall be recognized.***
> *(2) Into money or into property not similar or related in service or use to the converted property, the gain (if any) shall be recognized. . . .* [Emphasis added.]

The term "gain," of course, refers to the amount of reimbursement (in money or property) that exceeds the convertee's adjusted cost basis.

The period within which the converted property must be replaced (for nonrecognition of gain purposes) is a minimum of two years. It can be longer if based on reasonable cause and approved by the IRS. However, there is a period of "ambiguous starting time" depending on which comes first: destruction, disposition, threat, or condemnation. If you have investment property that has appreciated significantly before its conversion, you may want to replace it with similar property, to avoid tax.

Introduction to Form 4797

As a tax knowledgeable investor, there is an important auxiliary form of which you should be aware. It is second in importance only to Schedule D (Form 1040). [Recall Chapter 4.] It is **Form 4797: Sales of Business Property**. It attaches to your 1040 just like Schedule D.

Form 4797 is a catchall for most of the special situations that we have covered in this chapter plus some that we haven't covered. We call it the "when-in-doubt" form. Its format is comparable to Schedule D. So long as your entries in Columns (g) LOSS and (h) GAIN are computationally correct, you can pretty well report any transaction that does not properly go on Schedule D. In fact, many official supporting forms and schedules direct you to Form 4797 rather than to Schedule D.

Form 4797 is really a very useful form. It consists of three principal parts, namely:

Part I   —   Sales or Exchanges: Property Held More Than One Year
Part II   —   Ordinary Gains and Losses
Part III   —   Gain From Disposition of Recapture Property

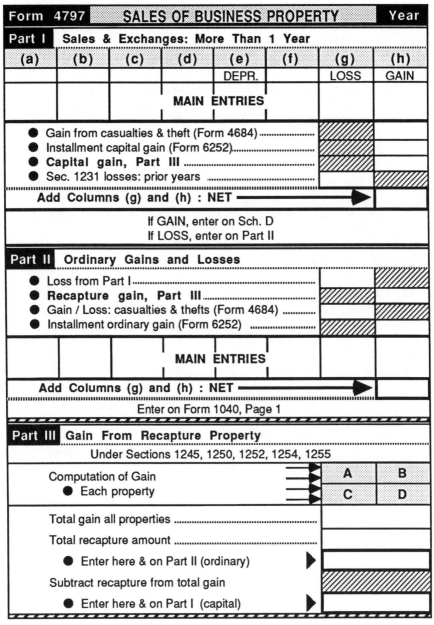

Fig. 9.3 - General Arrangement of Form 4797: Parts 1, II, and III

Parts I and II are on page 1 of the form, whereas Part III is on page 2. We have assembled all three parts into one highly abbreviated depiction in Figure 9.3. We just want you to get the functional substance of the form . . . for "awareness" reasons.

Part I of Form 4797 is a recapitulation of all Section 1231-type transactions, plus involuntary conversions, plus nonrecaptured 1231 net losses. There are provisions in Part I from transferring entries from Part III, from Form 4684 (Casualties and Thefts), and from Form 6252 (Installment Sales). If there is a net gain in Part I, you are directed onto Schedule D. If there is a net loss, you are directed onto Part II.

Part II is a recapitulation of all other transactions not reported in Part I or Part III, and not reportable on Schedule D. If there is net gain or loss in Part II, you are directed onto page 1 of Form 1040 to the line which reads—

Other gains or (losses) (Attach Form 4797)

In essence, Form 4797 splits your entries into two directions. One direction is to Schedule D; the other direction is to Form 1040 itself. Eventually, Schedule D directs you back to page 1 of Form 1040 to the line which reads—

Capital gain or (loss) (Attach Schedule D)

We believe that Form 4797 is so important that we urge you to get a copy of its latest official version. You should keep it as a reference source in your investment files at all times. Its four pages of official instructions are enlightening. The instructions could lead you into other investment possibilities that we have not even discussed.

10

TREATMENT OF GAINS

Schedule D (Form 1040) Is Where You Report, Separately, Most Capital Transactions (Sales, Exchanges, Etc.) For The Year. Directly Or Indirectly, Each Gain/Loss Computation Winds Up In A Column Headed Either LOSS Or GAIN. If Long-Term, Slightly Lower (Preferential) Tax Rates Apply. Certain Dispositions (Section 1231, Recapture, Involuntary Conversions) Require The Use Of Form 4797. Its Thrust Is To Re-Characterize As Many Transactions As Possible Into Ordinary Gain Where, On Form 1040, Regular (Nonpreferential) Rates Apply.

For a given year, it is the *net* capital gains which are subject to tax. This implies that there can be more than one sale transaction. There may be multiple sales, some of which produce gains and some of which produce losses. These gains and losses are netted against each other to arrive at — for purposes of this chapter — the net gains.

There are also net *ordinary* gains. These derive from certain capital transactions whose tax character is changed by virtue of the recapture-of-benefit rules presented in Chapter 9: Special Situations. Recapture gains, although called "ordinary," are not treated the same as ordinary earnings and profits from a trade or business. The earnings and profits from a trade or business are subject to social security tax on the owners thereof. In contrast, investors deriving ordinary gains (as well as capital gains) pay no social security tax on their gains.

The term "gains" applies to capital transactions only: that is, the net gain (capital and/or ordinary) derived from the sale, exchange, or other disposition of investment property.

Except for a year in which there is only one sale, individual transactions are not separately taxed. Each transaction is separately reported, and its gain or loss separately noted. However, it is the *aggregate* of the gains and losses to which the tax treatment applies.

The treatment of gains is going to differ, depending on the year of computation. This is because of the Tax Reform Act of 1986. That Act introduced major changes in capital gain treatment. The idea then was to reduce the preferential treatment of capital gains and force more recharacterization into ordinary gains.

In this chapter we will focus on the treatment of gains; in the next chapter we will focus on losses.

Page 1: Form 1040

Regardless of the number, type, and frequency of capital transactions you make for the year, the net gains (or net losses) wind up on page 1 of your Form 1040. They wind up as single-entry figures on one or more of three lines, namely:

Capital gain or (loss) [Schedule D]
Capital gain distributions
Other gains or (losses) [Form 4797]

It so happens that these three lines are clustered together in the mid-portion of the INCOME summary on page 1 (Form 1040). The effect is that they combine directly with other sources of income (or loss) that you may have for the taxable year.

Without using official line numbers (we're using sequential numbers), we list all tax-characterized sources of income in Figure 10.1. We show the gain/loss "investment cluster" in bold print.

Once on page 1, there is no distinction between your gain/loss from investment transactions and your other income. The tax distinction applies *before* your sale, etc. entries go on page 1.

Regarding the center of the cluster — capital gain distributions, if any — we should make a clarifying comment now. As we explained in Chapter 6: Portfolio Assets, capital gain distributions are dividends from regulated investment companies (mutual funds). They are paid or credited to your account without any decision, choice, or action on your part. These distributions are reported to

FORM 1040	U.S. Individual Income Tax Return	Year

● Your Name	Your Soc.Sec.No.
● Spouse's Name	Spouse's Soc.Sec.No.

☐ Filing Status and Exemptions   ☐ ☐ ☐ ☐

		Item	Amount
INCOME SUMMARY	1	Wages, salaries, tips, etc.	
	2	Taxable interest income : Sch. B	
	3	Dividend income : Sch. B	
	4	Taxable refunds of state income taxes	
	5	Alimony received	
	6	Business income or (loss) : Sch. C	
"Investment Cluster"	7	Capital gain or (loss) : Sch. D	
	8	Capital gain distributions	
	9	Other gains or (losses) : Form 4787	
	10	Taxable IRA distributions	
	11	Taxable pensions and annuities	
	12	Rents, royalties, partnerships, etc.: Sch. E	
	13	Farm income or (loss) : Sch. F	
	14	Unemployment compensation	
	15	Taxable social security benefits	
	16	Other income (list type and amount)	
		ADD all of the above. . . . . . **TOTAL INCOME** ▶	

Fig. 10.1 - The Income Items on Page 1, Form 1040

you on Form 1099-DIV (recall Figure 6.5), and you in turn report them on dividend Schedule B, Part II.

On Schedule B (Form 1040), Part II, there is a subtotal line which reads:

Capital gain distributions. Enter here and on Schedule D*

The asterisk (*) refers you to an official footnote which reads—

If you received capital gain distributions but do not need Schedule D to report any other gains or losses . . . enter those distributions on [page 1, Form 1040].

If you have no other capital transactions for the year (requiring neither Schedule D nor Form 4797), and are a mutual fund (portfolio) investor only, you'll have just one entry in the investment cluster on page 1. Your investment life is really simple. Chances are, however, you are probably paying maximum tax.

Schedule D Revisited

Even as a staid mutual fund investor, there comes a time for changing from one fund to another, from one portfolio to another, or for redeeming some of your shares. The moment you incur one capital transaction — transferring money from one account to another — you trigger the need for Schedule D: Capital Gains and Losses. Whether you incur one transaction or 10, Schedule D is needed. Whether the transaction is simple or complex, Schedule D is needed.

Regardless of which tax year is involved, the purpose of Schedule D (Form 1040) is the same. It is a summary format for ascertaining the net capital gain (or net capital loss) for that year. Where there is a net gain, the taxable amount thereof is set forth. (Where there is a net loss, the tax recognized amount is prescribed.)

Schedule D is not a tax computation form on its own. This is why it has to be attached to Form 1040. Form 1040 is the tax computation form. Hence, Schedule D is part of the *foundation base* for computing one's federal tax each year.

All capital transactions, either directly or indirectly, are entered on Schedule D. Ordinarily, there is a sufficient number of lines thereon to accommodate 10 transactions short-term and 10 transactions long-term. If the number of transactions exceeds the lines available, additional forms — continuation sheets — are used. A continuation sheet: Schedule D-1 will accommodate 45 transactions short-term and 45 transactions long-term. Thus, Schedules D and D-1 should take care of the great majority of cases, even for those who switch their investments frequently.

For summary instructional purposes, the essence of Schedules D and D-1 for each transactional entry is presented in Figure 10.2. The reference to Columns (a), (b), (c), etc. are those on the official form. We have purposely rearranged these columns into a

ITEM	HEADING	COMMENT
Column (a)	Description of property	Use self-explanatory abbreviations. Example: 29 sh XYZ, Inc.; 5.6 ac land; 3 contr. sugar.
Column (b)	Date Acquired	By purchase or other acquisition. Show month, day, year.
Column (c)	Date Sold	Sale, exchange, or other disposition. Show month, day, year.
Column (d)	Gross sales proceeds	Must correspond with Form 1099-B or equivalent. Make separate entry for each separate transaction.
Column (e)	Cost or other basis	"Cost when sold". Initial cost plus cumulative adjustments including capital expenses and indexing.
Column (f)	LOSS	If Col. (e) more than (d), subtract (d) from (e). Enter as loss.
Column (g)	GAIN	If Col. (d) more than (e), subtract (e) from (d). Enter as gain.

Fig. 10.2 - The Main "Direct Entries" on Schedule D (1040)

horizontal format so that we can present comments for each columnar entry. We urge you to read carefully the "Comment" portion of Figure 10.2. Columns (d) and (e) are your *make-or-break* entries on Schedule D. We have discussed these items previously in Chapters 2 through 5.

To give you a quick overview of the mechanics of Schedule D, we list below (for illustration purposes) five sequential sales. The loss or gain for each sale is shown in columnar form, corresponding to Columns (f) and (g) on Schedule D. The illustrative sales with their subtotaling and netting are:

	Loss	Gain
Sale #1		$ 3,500
Sale #2	$1,890	
Sale #3		10,860
Sale #4	5,820	
Sale #5	_____	26,200

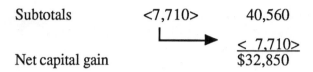

Subtotals	<7,710>	40,560
Net capital gain		< 7,710>
		$32,850

There is one fundamental and important message in the illustration above. That is, for a given taxable year, losses offset gains . . . dollar for dollar. Consequently, an investment loss becomes a tax benefit when you have sufficient overriding gains.

Nine "Dovetailing" Forms

Figure 10.2 lists the direct-entry columns on Schedule D. There are also indirect entries which are computed on other forms, with instructions for transferring into Columns (f) Loss and (g) Gain, as applicable. We listed these indirect-entry forms back in Figure 4.4. We re-list them here for review purposes. There are ten such "dovetailing" forms, namely:

1099-DIV	Capital gain distributions
2119	Gain from personal residence
4684	Gain from casualties & thefts
4797	Gain from Section 1231 sales
6252	Gain from installment sales
6781	Gain/loss: contracts & straddles
8824	Gain/loss: like-kind exchanges
K-1 (1041)	Gain/loss: estates & trusts
K-1 (1065)	Gain/loss: partnerships
K-1 (1120S)	Gain/loss: Sub S corporations

Each of the ten form types has its own characteristic entries for computing the net gain or net loss for each investment. The *aggregate* of the gains or losses for *each form type* is entered on Schedule D. It is possible to have more than one form of each type: the K-1's are the most susceptible. Once the aggregation is done for each form type, the entries go on Schedule D. There the subtotaling and netting follow the 5-sale illustration above.

Of the ten forms listed, five transfer gain only, and five transfer gain or loss. Because of the loss transference of these latter forms, we urge that you complete these forms first. As we've stated several times previously, the IRS's computer-matching effort is not going to pick up your loss transferences: only your gains.

We have not discussed previously, nor do we intend to now, Form 2119: Sale of Your Home. Ordinarily, one does not buy his personal residence solely as an investment. However, if it is sold at a gain, the gain is taxable. But if it is sold at a loss, the loss is not tax recognized.

A word or two about installment sales: Form 6252. This form applies only to gains: not losses. With Form 6252, it is possible to spread your taxable gain out over the period of the installment note that you received when closing the sale. Secured installment notes are often used when selling investment real estate. This is because of the quite large amount of money involved ($100,000 to $1,000,000 or more) and the nondivisible nature of realty assets. The key to installment sale tax benefits is the computation of a GPP — Gross Profit Percentage — which Form 6252 does for you. You apply the GPP each year to the installment payments on principal (*not* interest) that you receive. This means that each year you prepare a "continuing" Form 6252 and transfer the GPP gain to Schedule D.

Short-Term, Long-Term

As you are surely aware by now, Schedule D (and also Schedule D-1) is partitioned into two principal parts: I and II. Part I is officially designated—

Short-Term: Assets Held One Year or Less

Part II is officially designated—

Long-Term: Assets Held More Than One Year

If you follow the official instructions on Schedule D, each part is separately subtotaled and netted on its own. Then the instructions tell you to combine the net of Part I with the net of Part II. The end result is a net-net for the year — a single figure.

To see how the instructions work numerically, let's go back to our five illustrative sales above. Let us designated Sales #1, #2, and #3 as "short-term," and Sales #4 and #5 as "long-term." When we do so, the net-netting results are presented in Figure 10.3. We picked numbers so that we deliberately ended with a net capital gain. We did so because the focus in this chapter is on the treatment of net gains.

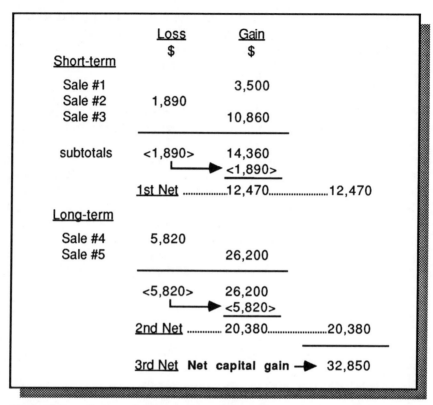

Fig. 10.3 - Selected Illustrative Sales Showing Net Capital Gain

Now that you have (in Figure 10.3) the general net-netting idea, we want to update you on some of the dovetailing forms listed above.

The instructions on some of the dovetailing forms direct you to transfer your net figures to either Part I or Part II of Schedule D. For example, Form 6781 (Gains and Losses From Section 1256 Contracts and Straddles) specifically says (for contracts)—

Enter 40% of net gain (or loss) as short-term on Schedule D
Enter 60% of net gain (or loss) as long-term on Schedule D

Similarly, each of the various K-1's (1041, 1065, and 1120S) has two separate instructional lines which read—

Net short-term capital gain (loss): Enter on Schedule D
Net long-term capital gain (loss): Enter on Schedule D

In contrast, certain dovetailing forms direct transference to Part II (Long-Term) of Schedule D only. For example, if you will look at an official Schedule D, you will **not** find in Part I (Short-Term) any entry line designated as: "Capital gain distributions." Said entry line appears only in Part II.

And then we have Form 4797: Sales of Business Property. Part I of that form is titled: Sales or Exchanges — Property Held More Than 1 Year. Thus, if you have a net gain here, you are instructed—

Enter the (net) gain as long-term capital gain on Schedule D

There is no provision whatever on For 4797 for short-term capital gain. Any short-term gain is automatically recharacterized as ordinary gain.

The "Cross-Netting" Scheme

"What is all of this short-term, long-term nomenclature all about?" you ask.

This brings us to the second fundamental and important message concerning the mechanics of Schedule D. Not only must you read all instructional lines carefully, for both your direct and indirect entries, you have to *cross-net* short-term with long-term, and losses with gains, before arriving at your net capital gain on Schedule D.

A depiction of the "cross-netting" that takes place on Schedule D is presented in Figure 10.4. A quick glance at Figure 10.4 should give you the general idea. The bottom line net may be all short-term, all long-term, or some combination of each.

Why in the world does Congress — and the IRS — drive you through all the machinations depicted in Figure 10.4?

Because there is a carrot-and-stick intention to provide preferential tax rates for net **long-term** capital gains. By "preferential" we mean: lower — at least slightly lower — tax rates for long-term gains than for short-term gains. The idea is to encourage making investments for the long term, thereby stabilizing the national economy and employment.

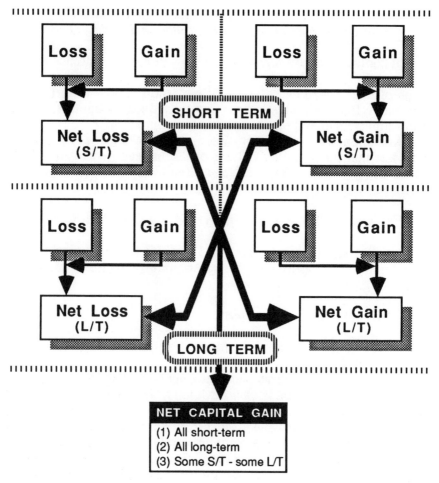

Fig. 10.4 - The "Cross-Netting" of Gains and Losses on Sch.D

Preferential Rate History

Giving preferential rates to long-term capital gains goes back many years to 1954. Between then and 1976, the treatment of gains was prescribed in tax code Section 1202: *Deduction for Capital Gains*. Instead of a rate reduction, the preferential treatment was in the form of an off-the-top deduction before applying the regular income tax rates. The pre-1976 rule read:

In the case of a taxpayer other than a corporation, if for any taxable year the net long-term gain exceeds the net short-term capital loss, 50 percent of the amount of such excess shall be a deduction from gross income.

In those years (1954-1976), "long term" meant more than six months. The maximum ordinary tax rates were 70%. Thus, with a 50% capital gain deduction, the effective maximum rate on capital gains (net long-term) was 35% (that is, 50% x 70%).

Between 1976 and 1978, various "pass-through" (conduit) entities — estates, trusts, partnerships, S corporations, mutual funds — were included in the preferential treatment as "other than a corporation." In 1978, "long term" was increased to more than one year and the capital gain deduction was increased to 60%. Section 1202(a) then read—

If for any taxable year a taxpayer other than a corporation has a net capital gain, 60 percent of the amount of the net capital gain shall be a deduction from gross income.

Between 1978 and 1982, there was a lot of backing and filling by Congress as to what length of time constituted long term. At one point it was back to six months, then to nine months, and again 12 months. During this period, the maximum ordinary rates remained at 70%. With the 60% capital gain deduction, the effective maximum rate on capital gains became 28% (that is, 40% x 70%).

In 1982, the maximum ordinary tax rates were reduced to 50%. This meant that the effective maximum rate on capital gains was reduced to 20% (that is, 40% x 50%).

The whole idea of an off-the-top deduction for capital gains was jettisoned in 1986. In that year, tax code Section 1202 was repealed outright. In its place, a *transitional* maximum rate on capital gains was set at 28%, with complete phase-out in 1988.

Between 1986 and 1990, more Congressional backing and filling took place re capital gains treatment. In 1990, the preferential difference between the maximum capital gains rate and the maximum ordinary tax rate was narrowed to a mere 3% (28% vs. 31%, respectively). Whether this preferential capital gains rate is substantially long-term motivating remains to be seen.

Form 4797 Revisited

Our short history above on capital gain rates is intended to make you more aware of Form 4797: Sales of Business Property. Although we introduced this form to you in Chapter 9: Special Situations, and we made a few passing comments on it in this chapter, we want to add still more to your store of knowledge on this second most important tax form . . . for investors.

Form 4797 has some of the format similarities to Schedule D. Its Parts I and II are labeled respectively as—

Part I: Sales or Exchanges — Property Held More than 1 Year

Part II: Ordinary Gains and Losses

Each part accommodates both direct and indirect entries. Whereas Schedule D has seven columns of direct entries: (a) through (g), Form 4797 has eight columns: (a) through (h). The additional column is headed:

Depreciation allowed (or allowable) since acquisition.

Depreciation is a tax benefit for property used in business or for the production of (rental) income. Depreciation is subject to recapture upon sale of that property. Otherwise the Loss/Gain columns of Form 4797 follow the same subtotaling and netting procedures of Schedule D.

As to the indirect entries on Form 4797, there are only four, namely:

Form 4684: Gain/loss from casualties and thefts
Form 6252: Gain from installment sales
Form 8824: Gain from like-kind exchanges
Part III (4797): Gain from recapture property

These entries appear in both Parts I and II. Part I is clearly long-term. Part II, however, is characterized as neither long nor short. It (Part II) includes *all* recapture gains regardless of holding period, all short-term capital gains, and all other ordinary gains and losses.

Form 4797 is designed to accommodate three principal categories of investor dispositions. These are—

One. Dispositions of section 1231 property
— that used in a trade or business by conduit entities, rental/royalty real estate, and involuntary conversions.

Two. Disposition of recapture property
— only if gains, where prior tax benefits were currently expensed.

Three. Dispositions of "unspecified" property
— "when in doubt" and not properly includible on Schedule D, such as foreclosure actions, default on debt, court judgments, etc.

To help you better understand and appreciate the versatility of Form 4797, we portray in Figure 10.5 its functional "mechanics."

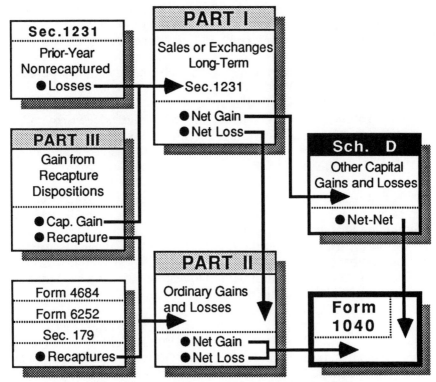

Fig. 10.5 - The Functional "Mechanics" of Form 4797

As we try to show, Section 1231 property benefits the most. It gets the best of both tax worlds: *capital gain* treatment if a net gain (in Part I); *ordinary loss* treatment if a net loss (in Part II). If you enter unspecified transactions in Part II, resulting in a net loss, they, too, get ordinary loss treatment. As you will see in the next chapter, ordinary loss treatment is more favorable than capital loss treatment.

Why "Ordinary" Gains?

From the IRS's point of view, the primary purpose of Form 4797 is to recharacterize as many of your disposition gains as possible into ordinary gain, rather than capital gain. This is the sole thrust of Part III, Form 4797: *Gain From Disposition of Property Under Section 1245, 1250, 1252, 1254, and 1255.* Under these sections, certain prior deduction allowances which were expensed (such as depreciation, depletion, amortization, mine exploration, intangible drilling, soil and water conservation, excludable cost sharings, etc.) are "recaptured" and recharacterized as ordinary gains.

Recapture and recharacterization are also adjunctive purposes of Parts I and II. In Part I, recapture targets your prior years nonrecaptured Section 1231 losses, if any. In Part II, recapture focuses on Form 4684 (casualties and thefts), Form 6252 (installment sales), and Section 179 dispositions (depreciable assets expensed under a special $10,000 annual election).

Why does the IRS go to so much effort to force many of your investment gains into ordinary income?

For starters, the tax rate on ordinary gain is higher than on capital gain. For the same total dollar gain in a property disposition, more revenue is generated through ordinary gains than capital gains.

Another reason is that there is less opportunity for loss offsets against ordinary gains than against capital gains. If you look back at Figure 10.1, at entries other than the investment cluster, what are the opportunities for offsetting losses?

Very few. Three, to be exact.

The only potential loss offsets against ordinary gains are Schedule C (sole business proprietorships), Schedule E (rents, royalties, partnerships), and Schedule F (farming and fishing). On all of these schedules, if there is a bottom line net loss, you must answer the **at-risk** question and complete Form 6198: At-Risk Limitations, as applicable. The complexity of this form alone discourages one from claiming his allocable losses.

If you have repetitive losses on Schedules C, E, and F, you'd promptly be challenged under the rules of Section 183: Activities Not Engaged In For Profit. Furthermore, any losses on page 1 of Form 1040 totaling 25% or more of your total positive income (on page 1), is a guaranteed target for IRS attack. Consequently, Form 4797 is biased towards producing positive entries (ordinary gain) on page 1 rather than negative entries.

The 1990 "Reconciliation" Act

Even when disposition gains can be properly classed as capital gain, a lot of tax begrudging goes on. Any preferential (lower) tax rates for net capital gains are always a target of envy from noninvestor taxpayers. Fortunately, the 1990 "Revenue Reconciliation Act" attempts to preserve at least a modicum of preferential difference between capital gains and ordinary gains.

The reconciliation effort, in effect, reinstates the 1987 "phased-out" 28% maximum rate on capital gains. This contrasts with the 31% to 33% effective maximum rates on ordinary income and gains. True, this differential is not great, but it is an effort to preserve the concept of preferential treatment.

Tax code Section 1(h): **Maximum capital gains rate**, as modified by the 1990 Act reads essentially as follows:

If a taxpayer has a net capital gain [the excess of net long-term capital gain over net short-term capital loss, if any] *for any taxable year then the tax imposed on such a taxpayer shall not exceed* **the sum of:**
  (1) a tax computed at the taxpayer's regular rates on **the greater of—**
  (A) taxable income reduced by the amount of net capital gain, or
  (B) the amount of taxable income that is taxed at a rate below 28%; **plus**
  (2) a tax of 28% on the amount of taxable income in excess of the amount determined in (1). [Emphasis added.]

This rather complex wording requires a whole new alternative tax computation subschedule on Schedule D. This is Part IV titled: *Tax Computation Using Maximum Capital Gains Rate* (of 20%). A total of nine computational steps is required.

To offset this Part IV complexity, proponents of preferential treatment have suggested a reinstatement of the pre-1987 concept of an outright capital gain *deduction*. This time, a graduated deduction has been proposed, such as:

1-year gain	a 10% deduction
2-year gain	a 20% deduction
3-year gain	a 30% deduction

As has been found in the past (1954 through 1986), the administration of tax law is simplified by allowing a capital gain deduction, rather than prescribing an alternative maximum tax rate. It is computationally easier to use deductions instead of addressing "the sum of," "the greater of," "or . . . plus." Hence, the saga of preferential treatment of net long-term capital gain is not over yet.

Three Benefits Retained

Even if there is no significant reinstatement of preferential rates for capital gains, there are still some tax benefits which remain. There are three such benefits . . . albeit modest.

The first benefit is the net-netting of capital losses with capital gains. As an ongoing investor, this feature alone permits you to clean up your investment inventory and get rid of your underperforming assets. You can sell the bad with the good, to obtain the tax "blend" that you want.

The second benefit is that there is no Social Security/Medicare tax to pay on your net capital gains. This tax is now a major — and growing — burden on all taxpayers generating personal service income. It's probably safe to say that capital gains will never be social security taxed. If they were to be so taxed, what would happen if there were net losses instead of gains? Would there be a social security tax *rebate* for capital losses?

The third benefit is one of timing and choice. As an investor, you choose when/what to buy and when/what to sell. With other sources of taxable income, you do not have so free a choice.

As an overall summary, therefore, capital gains do provide some tax benefits — if, indeed, there is a net gain.

11

TREATMENT OF LOSSES

Taxwise, There Are Two Kinds Of Investment Losses: CAPITAL And ORDINARY. Capital Losses Derive From The Cross-Netting Of All Entries (Including Gains) On Schedule D. The Deductibility Of Net Capital Losses Is Limited To $3,000 Per Year. Losses In Excess Of This Amount Are "Carried Over." Ordinary Losses Derive From The Net-Netting Of All Entries (Including Gains) On Form 4797. There Is No Per Year Limit To The Deductibility Of Ordinary Losses. However, If Your Form 4797 Losses Are Substantial Enough, The Result Could Be A "Net Operating Loss," Thereby Invoking Carrybacks And Carryforwards.

The treatment of net capital losses is a distinctly different phenomenon from the treatment of net capital gains. Whereas capital gains are recognized without limit, the tax recognition of capital losses is limited. The loss limitations are quite severe, as you will become aware in this chapter.

Let us illustrate the severity of the limitations in simplistic terms. Glance back briefly at Figure 10.3 and mentally reverse the loss/gain columnar amounts. Instead of a net capital gain of $32,850 we have a net capital *loss* of $32,850. Not every investor is fortunate to always have capital gains.

The "system" recognizes and taxes the full $32,850 gain. But if the $32,850 is a net loss, the system only recognizes $3,000 of that loss. That is, the tax-recognized loss (for offsetting other sources of Form 1040 income) is limited to $3,000 each current year. The unrecognized amount ($29,850 in this case) is carried over to subsequent tax years. If there were no capital gains and losses in the carryover years, one would have to carry his $29,850 loss for 10 years!

There is irony — and injury — in the limitations on losses. The IRS ignores all capital loss amounts which are reported to it on tax information returns: the K-1's and the like. Furthermore, losses do not show up in the gross sales proceeds which are reported to the IRS on Forms 1099-B, 1099-S, or equivalents. The message here is clear. The IRS is *not your helper* when it comes to capital (or other) losses. Each investor, therefore, has to diligently keep track of his own losses and enter them properly on his current- and subsequent-year returns.

"The Law" on Point

The specific tax law which addresses capital losses is Section 1211. Its official heading is: **Limitation on capital losses.** Subsection (b) thereof is titled "Other taxpayers." This means individuals and others than a corporation.

Section 1211(b) specifically addresses the subject of net capital losses for individuals. The entire section reads—

*In the case of a taxpayer other than a corporation, losses from sales or exchanges of capital assets shall be allowed only to the extent of the gains from such sales or exchanges, plus (if such losses exceed such gains) the **lower** of—*

(1) $3,000 ($1,500 in the case of a married individual filing a separate return), or
(2) the excess of such losses over such gains. [Emphasis added.]

The statute seems pretty clear: $3,000 net loss limit (period). If married, you can't increase this limit to $6,000 by filing separate returns. By statute, each spouse filing separately is limited to $1,500 in net capital loss. This $1,500 married-separate limit is often overlooked during the haste of tax preparation at tax time.

On Schedule D (1040), the capital loss limit computation shows up as follows:

Step 1 — *Combine lines ____ and ___, and enter net gain or (loss) here*   _____

Step 2 — *If* [Step 1] *is a (loss), enter here and as a loss on Form 1040, the **smaller** of:*   (_____)
    a. *The (loss) on* [Step 1]*; or*
    b. *($3,000) or, if married filing a separate return, ($1,500).*

What is the essence of the above?

It is that if your net capital loss for the year is $3,000 or less (for single, head of household, or married filing jointly), you can use up to that amount to offset other sources of income on Form 1040.

What we are talking about here are **net** capital losses (for a given year). That is, after all Schedule D gains, if any, have been taken into account. This is the cross-netting process — in reverse — that we depicted back in Figure 10.4. In this chapter, the Schedule D end result is a net loss, rather than a net gain. This net loss is that which appears in Part III of Schedule D: Summary of Parts I and II.

Within a given year, if there are any capital gains, the tax-recognized capital losses may be the amount of those capital gains *plus* $3,000. For example, suppose you have $25,000 in capital gains for the year. If applicable, you could write off on Schedule D as much as $28,000 in capital losses. The net/net would be $3,000 loss to write off against non-Schedule D sources of (positive) income.

If More Than $3,000 Loss

Suppose your net capital loss for the year is more than $3,000. Do you lose the excess loss over $3,000?

No; you do not.

There is a carryforward feature which allows you to write off the unused capital loss in future years. The carryforward feature goes on indefinitely . . . or until you die. If you are married (filing jointly), and your spouse dies, you can still carry forward the unused loss until you die. At that point, any still unused capital loss carryforward becomes a "loss/loss." It cannot be picked up and deducted on your death tax (estate) return.

The amount of capital loss carryforward *each year* is limited to $3,000 plus any offsetting capital gains. It is a repetitive process:

$3,000 net loss write-off each year, until the total net capital loss (for the computational year) is used up.

The tax law on point is Section 1212(b): **Capital loss carrybacks and carryovers.** This section is substantially more complex than the $3,000 loss limit section above. So, we'll present the carryforward feature first. Carryforwards (carryovers) are far more applicable to ordinary investors than carrybacks.

Section 1212(b)(1) reads in significant part as follows:

> *If a taxpayer other than a corporation has a net capital loss for any taxable year—*
> > *(A) the excess of the net short-term capital loss over the net long-term capital gain for such year shall be a short-term capital loss in the succeeding taxable year, and*
> > *(B) the excess of the net long-term capital loss over the net short-term capital gain for such year shall be a long-term capital loss in the succeeding taxable year.*

In other words, if you have a net capital loss in excess of $3,000 for a given year, you have to go back over your Schedule D, and determine which portion of the excess loss is short-term, and which portion is long-term. That is, you split the excess loss into its short-term and long-term components.

The main reason for the excess-loss split-up is that, computationally, the short-term losses are consumed first. Another reason is that the short/long split-up offers a better "blending" of the carryover rules with any excess losses that may have originated in prior years. Some investors have substantial unused losses which originated pre-1987 when long-term capital gains were treated so favorably. Hence, the rationale is that long-term losses should be used last.

If "Negative" Taxable Income

The carryover/carryforward rules above are based on the assumption that the taxpayer has positive taxable income, irrespective of his $3,000 loss from Schedule D. If he has other losses (current-year plus prior-year carryovers, if any) that do not appear on Schedule D, the taxpayer/investor — it could be you — might have *negative* taxable income. If this is the case, the amount of capital loss carryforward becomes a notch more complex.

The rule on point is Section 1212(b)(2): **Treatment of amounts under Section 1211(b)(2).** We refrain from quoting this statute because it will only confuse you. It says, in essence, that when one has a negative taxable income, the $3,000 loss limit is treated as capital *gain* and, together with the applicable personal exemption amounts, are used to compute an "adjusted taxable income." Then, the capital loss allowable for the year becomes **the lesser of—**

1. $3,000,
2. excess of losses over gains, **or**
3. adjusted taxable income.

The idea underlying Section 1212(b)(2) is to give you a slight break, by increasing your capital loss carryforward when you have an adjusted taxable income of less than $3,000. Ordinarily, with positive taxable income, you would consume $3,000 of your capital losses each year. But if you have negative taxable income, your tax-consumed amount may be something less than $3,000. It could even be zero! Anything less than $3,000 increases the recognized carryforward correspondingly.

For example, if your adjusted taxable income is $1,000, you consume only $1,000 of the $3,000 loss limit. This, correspondingly, increases your loss carryforward.

To illustrate, suppose you had $6,500 in net Schedule D losses. Your adjusted taxable income — after following official instructions to Form 1040 and Schedule D — is $1,000. Your loss carry-forward is $5,500 (6,500 - 1,000). Otherwise, your carryforward loss would be $3,500 (6,500 - 3,000).

To do the carryforward loss computations properly, Schedule D (Part V) instructs you through 19 entry lines. Yes, 19! This is why we refrained from quoting you Section 1212(b)(2). Incidentally, Part V of Schedule D is titled:

Part V: Your Capital Loss Carryovers
    A — Your Carryover Limit
    B — Short-Term Capital Loss Carryover
    C — Long-Term Capital Loss Carryover

Experienced capital loss investors (with positive taxable incomes) can do the carryforward computations in their heads. From Schedule D, they separate the net capital loss into short-term, long-term amounts. They subtract $3,000 first from the short-term component, and carry everything else forward. For record-keeping purposes, the last carryforward lines in subpart V-B (short-term) and V-C (long-term) should show the specific dollar amounts applicable.

Section 1256 Loss Carrybacks

If you are a sophisticated investor, you have probably engaged in Section 1256 contracts and straddles. We introduced this subject in Chapter 9: Special Situations. We also made reference therein to Form 6781: Gains and Losses From Section 1256 Contracts and Straddles. In Chapter 10 (Treatment of Gains), we cited the wording on Form 6781 to show how its short-term, long-term gains were transferred from Form 6781 to Schedule D.

With respect to Section 1256 losses, a special *carryback* rule applies. This rule — Section 1212(c) — is tax code titled: **Carryback of losses from section 1256 contracts to offset prior gains from such contracts.** This section consists of approximately 700 words. The gist is that you carry back your losses—

> *to each of the 3 taxable years preceding the loss year, and to the extent that . . . such loss is allowed as a carryback . . .*
> *(i) 40 percent . . . shall be treated as a short-term capital loss . . . and,*
> *(ii) 60 percent . . . shall be treated as a long-term capital loss.*

It is of particular interest to note that Section 1212(c) mandates the separation of short-term and long-term losses by prescribed percentages. In other loss transactions, you make the short-long separation from your actual entries on Schedule D.

Other portions of Section 1212(c) tell you that you must "coordinate" your carryback losses with the $3,000 per year computational limit on net capital losses in all forms. In other words, you cannot use Section 1256 carryback losses to exceed the $3,000 loss limit described above.

The 3-year carryback rule for Section 1256 losses is *elective*; it is not mandatory. The election is signified by checking a box on Form 6781 which reads—

☐   *Check here if you elect to carry back a net section 1256 contracts loss.*

If you elect the carryback provision, you go back three tax years on Schedule D and start working forward. If you do this, subsection 1212(c)(3) tells you that you can only use the carryback losses to offset Section 1256 gains (if any) that previously occurred in the carryback years. You cannot use Section 1256 carryback losses to offset non-section 1256 gains.

There is a very special reason why you are allowed to carry back losses on contracts and straddles. In the carryback years, before the loss carrybacks, you were forced to "mark-to-market" your unrealized gains (on unexpired and offsetting positions) at the end of each year. If you reported Section 1256 unrealized gains for the carryback years, you are entitled to reduce them for subsequent-year realized losses. You are not allowed this carryback feature for other capital transactions.

Pseudo-Transaction Losses

In most investor transactions, money, property, or other consideration change hands willingly at time of sale, exchange, or other disposition. In the case of contracts and straddles, "other consideration" is in the form of rights which have expired or are offsetting. There is also a category of investment activities which we label as "pseudo-transactions." These are situations where the consideration is so intangible that it produces outright capital losses. Such situations are—

1. Nonbusiness bad debts
2. Worthless securities
3. Voluntary conveyances
4. "Wash sale" transfers

There are times when an investor advances his money to a recipient agent for some express investment purpose. Subsequently, the recipient defaults and the investor's money vanishes. Efforts to retrieve it or the intended investment asset prove hopeless. This is called a *nonbusiness bad debt*. It is "nonbusiness" because the investor himself/herself is not in the trade or business of regularly lending money. It is a "bad debt" because the money advanced is never returned. Taxwise, nonbusiness bad debts are treated as short-term capital losses. This is so stated in Section 166(d)(1)(B): **Bad debts; Nonbusiness**. Consequently, the loss amount is entered in Part I of Schedule D.

There are times when a bona fide investment is made in stock or stock rights of a corporate enterprise. With the passage of time, the stock turns out to be a dud. It is totally worthless. No foul play need be involved. The venture behind the stock just didn't succeed in the market place. In the tax world, the designation *worthless securities* applies. Once you establish that the securities are indeed worthless, they are entered on Part II of Schedule D as a long-term capital loss. This is the gist of Section 165(g)(1): **Losses; Worthless securities**.

There are also times when the market value of investment property falls below its contract of indebtedness. Such "debt contracts" may be evidenced by promissory notes, deeds of trust, margin accounts, collateralized loans, etc. When market value falls below the debt owed, the property often is surrendered or abandoned, and the creditor takes it back either voluntarily or through foreclosure. This form of disposition is called *voluntary conveyance*. When this happens, the tax basis in the abandoned property is reduced by the amount of the actual debt relieved. The capital loss involved may be short-term or long-term, depending on the year of abandonment. This is the gist of Section 1017(a): **Discharge of indebtedness**.

For example, you bought a parcel of land for $10,000. You put down $1,500 and the seller financed the deal with a $8,500 deed of trust. The property declines in value to $7,500. You offer to convey it back to the seller, who accepts it and cancels the $8,500 deed of trust. Your capital loss is $1,500 (10,000 - 8,500). It is NOT the $10,000 purchase price, nor the $7,500 market value.

A *wash sale* is the selling of stock or securities for the purpose of taking a tax loss on Schedule D, with the express intention of reacquiring "substantially identical" stock shortly thereafter. If the reacquisition occurs within a period of 30 days before, or 30 days after, the disposition, the Schedule D loss is not tax recognized. That is, the transaction is disregarded in its entirety . . . until a bona fide sale occurs. This is the gist of Section 1091(a): **Loss from wash sales of stock or securities**.

All of the above *capital* losses, when net-netted and cross-netted for the year, are subject to the same $3,000 loss limit described earlier. As a summary in this regard, we present Figure 11.1. We

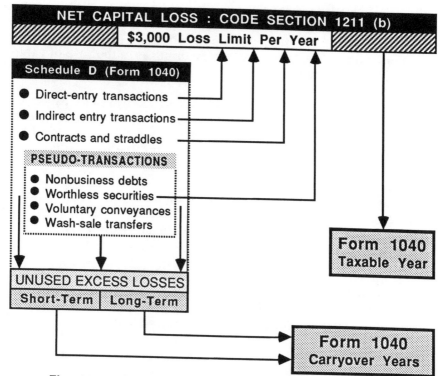

Fig. 11.1 - Depiction of the $3,000 Capital Loss Limit

want to move on now to the treatment of *ordinary* losses that can arise from certain investment transactions.

Section 1231 Losses

In Chapter 9: Special Situations, we touched on Section 1231 losses. We did so within the context of the recapture process, should subsequent Section 1231 dispositions produce gains instead of losses. In this chapter, we want to assume that we are dealing strictly with **net** Section 1231 losses, after taking into account any offsetting recapture for Section 1231 gains. Section 1231 property, recall, is that which is used in a trade or business (such as by conduit entities), or for the production of income (such as rental/royalty realty), or involved in involuntary conversion (by requisition, condemnation, or threat thereof).

The important point that we are leading up to is that Section 1231 losses are treated as ordinary losses: NOT capital losses. Taxwise, ordinary losses are more beneficial. The simple reason is that ordinary losses have no statutory limits as in the case of capital losses. In other words, the $3,000 net capital loss limit does not apply to ordinary losses.

The only limit to ordinary losses is a practical one. Since said losses combine directly with all non-Schedule D sources of income, the limitation is — should said losses be so great — the driving of one's taxable income negative. Negative taxable income produces zero tax. Zero taxable income also produces zero tax. The excess negative is not carryforwardable.

Unfortunately, in the tax code the statutory wording is not as direct as we have stated. The official wording is convoluted and fuzzy. One pertinent excerpt appears in subsection 1231(a)(2), namely—

If the section 1231 gains, for any taxable year, do not exceed the section 1231 losses for such taxable year, such gains and losses **shall not** *be treated as gains and losses from sales or exchanges of capital assets.* [Emphasis added.]

In plain language, this wording says that if there are net Section 1231 losses, they are not to be treated as capital losses.

How are such losses to be treated?

You have to read subsection 1231(a)4) and interpret its fuzzy wording, to wit—

The section 1231 losses shall be included only if and to the extent taken into account in computing taxable income, except that section 1211 shall not apply.

Section 1211, recall, is: Limitation on Capital Losses . . . at $3,000. The wording "taken into account in computing taxable income" means that the net 1231 loss **bypasses** Schedule D and goes — via Form 4797, Part II (Ordinary Gains and Losses) — onto Form 1040. Once on Form 1040, the losses combine directly with other income and losses to derive one's taxable income.

A schematization of how the net Section 1231 losses (noncapital) combine to produce taxable income is presented in Figure 11.2. Note that we show the Schedule D loss limit of

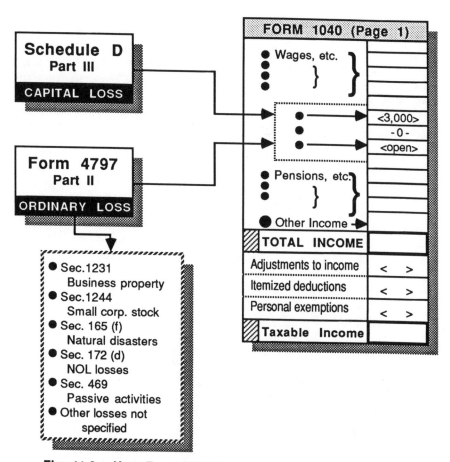

Fig. 11.2 - How Form 4797 Losses Combine on Form 1040

$3,000. Note that we also indicate that other ordinary losses can be accommodated on Form 4797: Sales of Business Property.

Section 1244 Losses

There are still other kinds of investment losses that are treated as ordinary (noncapital) losses. Foremost in this regard are Section 1244 losses. Section 1244 is titled: **Losses on small business stock**. Similar treatment is given to Section 1242 (Losses on small business investment company stock) and to Section 1243 (Loss of small business investment company).

A "small business corporation" is a trade or business entity whose total stock authorized and issued does not exceed $1,000,000 (1 million). To qualify for ordinary loss treatment, the corporation must issue specifically designated *Section 1244 stock*. This is a tax character designation: not a class of ownership. The tax-recognized losses on such stock cannot exceed $100,000 for married investors filing jointly, and $50,000 for single persons (or married filing separately). This is the maximum loss tax allowed for any given taxable year.

The citations on point are Sections 1244(a) and 1244(b). These sections, in pertinent part, read as follows:

(a) In the case of an individual, a loss on section 1244 stock issued to such individual or to a partnership which would (but for this section) be treated as a loss from the sale or exchange of a capital asset shall, to the extent provided [herein], *be treated as an **ordinary loss**.*
(b) For any taxable year the aggregate amount treated . . . as an ordinary loss shall not exceed—
(1) $50,000 or
(2) $100,000 in the case of a husband and wife filing a joint return for such year. [Emphasis added.]

In a Section 1244 loss situation, how would the ordinary loss be signified on your tax return?

It would *not* go on Schedule D. That is for capital losses only. It goes on Form 4797, Part II (Ordinary Gains and Losses).

If you will glance back at Figure 9.3, you will see that Part II has a section labeled "Main Entries." You enter in Column (a) the description: "Sec. 1244 stock." You then fill in the other applicable columns ending with the loss column (g). You proceed down the form to the instruction which directs you to page 1 of Form 1040. There, the ordinary loss amount offsets your other ordinary income without concern for the $3,000 capital loss limit.

Disaster Losses

Another category of investment losses that enter (indirectly) onto Form 4797, Part II pertains to disasters. A "disaster" is an area-wide destruction by natural causes. The causes may be wildfire, storm, flood, hurricane, tornado, earthquake, volcanic eruption, and the like. The area is so devastated that it warrants federal assistance under the Disaster Relief and Emergency Assistance Act. The "assistance" may not actually materialize, but it is "warranted" nevertheless.

Any form of investment property damaged or destroyed by a natural disaster is eligible for special loss treatment. About the only exception is the loss of debt obligations (such as bearer bonds, gold coins, traveler's checks) which have not been registered when otherwise required. The disallowance issue on registration-required assets is more a matter of proof of ownership. Otherwise, the owner/investor of any property destroyed can compute the tax-recognized loss on Section B of Form 4684: Casualties and Thefts. Then, one of the bottom lines on this form (there are several) instructs you to—

Enter the net gain or (loss) here and on Form 4797, Part II, at line _____.

If your computed disaster loss is substantial in amount, you have a special option. The option is subsection 165(i)(1): **Disaster losses; Election to take deduction for preceding year**. In other words, you can carry back a disaster loss one year. Regarding the carryback year, the tax code says—

If an election is made under this subsection, the casualty resulting in the loss shall be treated . . . as having occurred in the taxable year for which the deduction is claimed.

Disaster losses to investments can be quite substantial. This is because natural disasters are legal exceptions to general insurance coverage. A Beaufort 15 hurricane or a Richter 8 earthquake, for example, could wreak financial havoc with insurance companies themselves. There are certain risks in all investments, and natural disaster is one of them.

Net Operating Losses

If you invest in conduit assets (Chapter 7), rental real estate (Chapter 8), farm rentals (Chapter 9), or are involved in foreign expropriation losses, you are subject to special loss limitation rules. The two most prevalent such rules are:

> **Sec. 465** — Deductions limited to amounts at risk.
> **Sec. 469** — Passive activity losses and credits limited.

Both of these rules permit you to "suspend" — hold in abeyance — your cumulative unused losses until sale, exchange, or other fully taxable transaction (of the loss item) takes place.

When you final-dispose of a passive activity asset, the suspended losses are treated as *addition* to basis. This reduces your gain or increases your loss on the terminating transaction. Should a net loss result, the transaction is treated as a Section 1231 loss that goes onto Form 4797. Initially, the loss entry goes into Part I (Sales or Exchanges), where it combines with other gains and losses. If Part I results in a net loss, said loss is transferred to Part II for further netting. Recall Figure 10.5.

All Form 4797 net/net ordinary losses wind up on page 1 of Form 1040. We've stated this several times previously. What we haven't stated previously is that these losses — if large enough — can swamp all other sources of tax-reportable income. Should this happen a **negative** total income results. When there is a negative *total* income on Form 1040, you have what is called a "Net Operating Loss" (NOL) for that year. Net operating losses also receive special treatment.

The net operating loss (NOL) rules are set forth in tax code Section 172: **Net operating loss deduction**. Take care to note that an NOL is characterized as a "deduction." Section 172(a) specifically says—

> *There shall be allowed as a deduction for the taxable year an amount equal to the aggregate of (1) the net operating loss carryovers to such year, plus (2) the net operating loss carrybacks to such year.*

Now we are confronted with a barrage of NOL computations consisting of current-year losses, carryover losses, and carryback losses.

We will not go too deeply into Section 172. It is very complicated. It consists of approximately 5,600 statutory words plus endless pages of IRS regulations. However, the gist is that — after some rather elaborate calculations — you can carry an NOL back three years. If there is any remaining unused NOL, you can carry it forward for 15 years. Or, if you so elect, you can waive the carryback and carry the loss deduction forward only [Sec. 172(b)(3)(C)].

Elect NOL Carryforward

If you have a legitimate NOL loss, and it is substantial in amount, we suggest you elect the carryforward-only provision of subsection 172(b)(3). If you do so, you could be spared much aggravation by the IRS. NOL carryback computations are complicated and time-consuming. There are many opportunities for making errors. Consequently, the IR dislikes allowing NOL carryback deductions.

If you want the nth degree of maximum NOL deduction, you must comply rigorously with the 540-word "modification rule" of Section 172(d). But if you accept a simple, reasonably close approximation, your NOL is your *total income* in negative form. This approximate NOL comes from the straight-forward combination of all income/loss entries on page 1 of your Form 1040. (*Note*: Do not confuse total income with taxable income.)

We suggest, now, that you go back and review Figure 10.1. Look particularly at the **total income** block. If this is *negative*, you have an NOL to the extent of the negative amount. You can stop your return at this point, as there will be no income tax due.

For example, suppose your total income on page 1 of Form 140 turns out to be $66,830 negative or <$66,830>. This is your approximate NOL. It is probably off no more than 5 to 10% of the maximum allowable NOL, if you went through the rigors of Section 172(d): Modifications. Thus, we consider your NTI (negative total income) as being "close enough" to your NOL. It is certainly much simpler, and it tends to be on the conservative side.

If you go forward with your NTI/NOL to the next succeeding year or years, we suggest that the following notation be added to your Form 1040. In the white space just below the total income line, enter—

T/P elects Sec. 172(b)(3) NOL carryforward
[The "T/P" stands for "taxpayer": **you**]

This puts the IRS on notice that you are treating your NTI as your NOL, and that you intend to carry it forward rather than backward. The mechanics involved are illustrated in Figure 11.3.

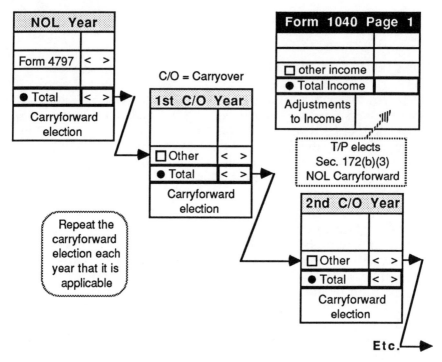

Fig. 11.3 - The NOL Carryforward Scheme on Form 1040

As depicted, in each succeeding year, you enter the unused carryover amount on the "other income" line. In the white space provided, enter "NOL carryforward," and show the amount either in parentheses ( ) or in brackets < > to designate that it is deduction. Note on any official Form 1040 that the *other income* line is just above the **total income** line on page 1. Any negative amount of other income is going to reduce your total income. This in turn will reduce your taxable income . . . and your tax.

12

WRAP-UP MATTERS

As A Serious Investor, You Need Familiarity
With Four Primary Tax Forms, Namely: (1)
Schedule D, (2) Form 4797, (3) Schedule E,
And (4) Schedule B. Be Aware Also Of The
Nominee Liabilities When Co-Investing With
Others. If You Sell Investment Property And
Finance The Buyer Yourself, You Have The
"Imputed Interest" Rule — Section 483 — To
Worry About. Interest And Dividends From
State And Local Bonds Are Income Tax
Exempt, As Are The Proceeds Of Life
Insurance At Death. Investing Globally
Through Sector Mutual Funds Provides All The
"Flavor" Of International Investing — Including
Paying Foreign Taxes.

In this chapter, we want to retouch on a few of the key points presented earlier. By doing so, we hope to impress on you the importance of certain tax forms for serious investors. Such forms are (1) Schedule D, (2) Form 4797, (3) Schedule E, and (4) Schedule B . . . in this order. Without at least some familiarity with these forms, you are at the "maximum revenue" mercy of the IRS.

We also want to present some new matters which we set aside previously, until more subject breadth and depth had been presented. For example, we want to touch on co-investor problems, seller financing, investment interest expense, tax-free bonds, and life insurance and annuities.

And, finally, we want to close this chapter — and this book — with a few words on global investing. As long as you are a U.S.

citizen (whether resident or not) **or** a U.S. resident (whether citizen or not), you are required to file U.S. Tax Form 1040. This is so, even though all of your gains and losses accrue outside of the United States. Investing today — and the tax accounting therewith — is a worldwide affair.

Determination of Gain or Loss

Gain or loss is measured at the time of disposition of property: not upon its acquisition. "Disposition" is the sale, exchange, or transfer of property from one legal owner to another legal owner. Disposition is the severance of all enjoyment and control over property previously held. At the moment of severance, the tax accounting ax falls.

The amount of gain or loss must be determinable. That is, the amount must be ascertained with definiteness, exactness, and conclusiveness. There can be no arbitrary or indecisive matters. The correct gain or loss must be specific; it must be traceable; it must be provable. There must be a "tax trail" (cost or other basis) and profit motive . . . all along the way.

While gains are always nice and losses are tax limited, there are situations in which "no loss whatsoever" is recognized. These occur when property is used for personal purposes, for hobby and recreational activities, for prearranged sham transactions, and for certain transactions between related taxpayers. While, cavalierly, you may consider these kinds of activities as "investments," they are IRS suspect at all times.

When establishing the correct gain or loss, the **burden of proof is on you**: the taxpayer/investor. It is never on the IRS. This is where your tax records and money trails come in. Without clear and convincing records, you are "tax dead."

If the correct gain or loss cannot be determined with certainty, the IRS will treat all proceeds from a disposition as *all gain*. No losses whatsoever will be recognized; no return of capital will be recognized. This presumption maximizes the tax burden on the disposer of property. This is the rationale for the broker reporting law — Section 6045 — requiring *gross proceeds* on Forms 1099-B and 1099-S.

Some investors naively believe that the IRS would not do this: would not tax the gross proceeds as all gain. Inexplicably, they assume that the IRS would make a conscientious effort to contact the broker on the taxpayer's behalf to establish the correct gain or loss.

In no way! It is not up to the IRS to do anything constructive. It's sole job is to collect maximum revenue . . . period.

Many investors are truly shocked when they learn that the IRS does indeed have the power to take arbitrary actions. The clearest statutory authority for doing so is Section 6020(b): **Authority of Secretary to Execute Return**. The term "Secretary" means the Secretary of the U.S. Treasury or his delegate, the Internal Revenue Service. A "return" is one or more transactions for which a tax accounting is required.

Section 6020(b) reads in part as follows—

If any person fails to make any return required by an internal revenue law or regulation made thereunder at the time prescribed therefor, . . . the Secretary shall make such return from his own knowledge or from such information as he can obtain through testimony or otherwise. Any return so made and subscribed by the Secretary shall be prima facie good and sufficient for all legal purposes.

Section 6020(b) has been tested in federal court and it stands. The judicial interpretation has been that the IRS need ascertain only one fact and, on that basis alone, can prepare a return. It is not required to ascertain all facts surrounding a controverted matter: just one fact only! Obviously, the IRS will pick the one fact that will maximize revenue, namely: the gross sales price.

So, there you have it. Either you determine the gain or loss correctly, or the IRS will make an assessment that will horrify you.

Four Important Forms

Your best protection against IRS's arbitrariness and abusiveness — in fact, your *only* protection — is the preparation and filing of **four** important tax forms. This is not to say that these are the only investor forms involved, but that they are important above all others. These four forms are:

1. Schedule D — Capital Gains and Losses
2. Form 4797 — Sales of Business Property
3. Schedule E — Supplemental Income and Loss
4. Schedule B — Interest and Dividend Income

Why are these forms important above others?

Because the net result on each of these forms transfers directly onto page 1 of your Form 1040. It is true that other investor forms supplement and dovetail into each of the four forms listed. But, if need be, you could omit (temporarily) the auxiliary forms and make your entries and notations directly on the four. At least you would have made adequate disclosures for computing your tax, even if you have to make amendments later.

What goes on each of the four forms?

For details, we urge that you go back and review the pertinent chapters thereon. For a nut-shell summary, though, we list the main contents of each form as follows:

Schedule D

Part I   — Short-Term Capital Gains and Losses
Part II   — Long-Term Gains and Losses
Part III   — Summary of Parts I and II
Part IV   — Maximum Capital Gains Rate
Part V   — Your Capital Loss Carryovers

Form 4797

Part I   — Sales and Exchanges and Involuntary Conversions
Part II   — Ordinary Gains and Losses
Part III   — Gain From Disposition of [Recapture] Property

Schedule E

Part I   — Income or Loss: Rentals and Royalties
Part II   — Income or Loss: Partnerships and S Corporations
Part III   — Income or Loss: Estates and Trusts
Part IV   — Income or Loss: Mortgage Investment Conduits
Part V   — Summary of Parts I Through IV

Schedule B

Part I   — Interest Income
Part II   — Dividend Income
Part III   — Foreign Accounts and Trusts

In Figure 12.1, we try to pull all the pieces together for you in schematic form. For reminder purposes only, we list (without

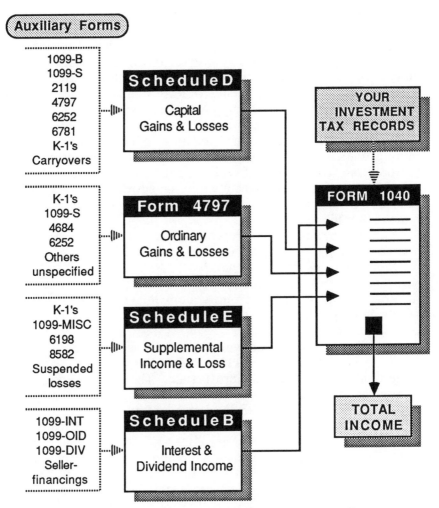

Fig. 12.1 - Your Most Important Investment Tax Forms

description) the auxiliary forms associated with each of the four primary forms.

We know you hate filling out and attaching tax forms. But we think you would hate more the devastation and injustice of the IRS taxing your gross proceeds.

INVESTOR GAINS & LOSSES

Co-Investor Reporting

Because of the maximum revenue goal of our tax system, you have particular tax accounting obligations when co-investing with others (other than your spouse and dependent children). It is common practice among friends, family members, and business associates to get together informally and pool money for some investment venture. It could be a lottery drawing, gambling pool, start-up of a new business, partnership interests, hot-tip stock, gold mining deal, land purchase, and so on. For obvious practical reasons, one person has to collect and handle the money, and commit to the intended investment. One person has to receive the proceeds therefrom, if any. Such a person becomes the agent or nominee for the others.

Should the investment produce any interest, dividends, proceeds, return of capital, discharge of indebtedness, or other distributions, guess what happens?

The payer reports to the IRS all proceeds and distributions on the nominee/agent's social security number. This means that if you are the nominee, you have to report on your return and pay full tax on your co-investors' money . . . UNLESS.

The first "unless" is that you as the nominee recipient submit to each co-participant a **Form W-9**: Request for Taxpayer Identification Number and Certification. The "certification" is the co-participant's signature — under penalties of perjury — that his or her social security number (SSN) is true and correct.

The second "unless" is that you prepare for each distributee the appropriate 1099 form, such as: 1099-INT, 1099-DIV, 1099-B, 1099-S, 1099-MISC. Then you prepare **Form 1096**: Annual Summary and Transmittal of U.S. Information Returns. To Form 1096, you attach the original of each of the 1099's and send them to the IRS. "Where to File" information is listed on the back of Form 1096. Of course, send a copy of each 1099 to each co-investor distributee.

The third "unless" is that if you have a recalcitrant or evasive distributee who avoids or refuses to give you his correct social security number, you must *withhold* from that distributee 20% of his/her share of the funds. This is required of you by Section 3406(a): **Backup withholding; Requirement to deduct and withhold**. When you withhold 20% of your associate's money, that person is not going to be very happy with you. It is either you withhold, or you pay his/her tax.

So, now you have several hundred or several thousand dollars of a co-investor's tax money. What do you do with it?

The instructions on point are not very clear. All you're told is: "pay to the IRS." Where? How? On what form? You can't just send a withholding check blithely to the IRS. It must be attached to some IRS form. Otherwise, it is put into a "suspense account" and no credit is given to you for your withholding effort.

Our suggestion is that you use Form 1096 (transmitting the 1099's), circle in heavy red the box labeled: *Federal income tax withheld*, attach an explanation and check payable to the IRS. When you sign the transmittal form, enter in the "title" space the word: *Nominee*. Be sure to photocopy Form 1096 and your withholding payment check, for later reconciliation with the IRS's computer inquiries.

As a quick guide to the co-investor accounting/reporting maze that you face, we present Figure 12.2. Perhaps, after you go through the Figure 12.2 exercise once, or if you are IRS-forced to pay tax on your co-investors' money, you may cease co-investing altogether.

Seller Financing: Section 483

Seller financing is a post-disposition matter with a certain special tax rule of its own. The rule — called "Section 483" — affects all sales and exchanges over $3,000 where the seller finances the transaction in whole or part. These are those deferred payment arrangements (installment sales) where the seller becomes a lender to the buyer.

Previously, we touched on installment sales and the necessity for preparing Form 6252: Installment Sale Income. The computations thereon address the installments on principal: NOT the interest payments associated therewith. Although the buyer makes a single payment, it is up to the seller to separate the principal and interest, and report each separately on his tax return. The payments on principal go on Form 6252. Where do the payments on interest go?

Installment interest received goes on Schedule B, Part I, line 1, where its says—

Interest income from seller-financed mortgages. (See instructions and list name of payer.)

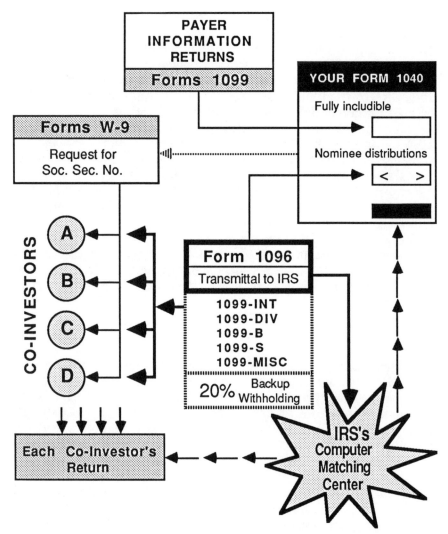

Fig. 12.2 - Nominee's Co-Investor Reporting Maze

What the instructions don't tell you is that there is a tax trap out there. The trap is Section 483: **Interest on certain deferred payments**. This section is called the "unstated" or *imputed interest* rule (about 850 words). The rule is fuzzily worded, as exemplified by the following excerpt:

(a) Amount constituting interest

. . . In the case of any payment . . . under any contract for the sale or exchange of any property . . . there shall be treated as interest that portion of the total unstated interest under such contract which . . . is properly allocable to such payment.

The tax trap is the phrase: "properly allocable to such payment." It applies to all deferred payment transactions maturing more than one year after the sale or exchange which either (1) do not provide for interest, or (2) provide for interest at below market rates.

For example, under distress conditions, you sold a parcel of land out in the boondocks for $10,000. You paid $15,000 for it. After several years of no takers, you accepted an offer of 5% down and $9,500 in installments at 5% per annum interest for 10 years. At the time, commercial interest rates were 10%. Thus, you've made a below-market-rate loan for which Section 483 applies.

Section 483 authorizes the IRS to impute interest on your installment note — at Applicable Federal Rates (AFR). The AFR's are based on the rate of interest paid on U.S. Treasury securities. The AFR's are published monthly by the IRS. They are applicable to all seller-financed sales and exchanges after 1984.

In our $9,500 installment note example above, suppose the AFR rate is 8.5%. Since you only charged the buyer 5%, your imputed interest is an additional 3.5%. This means that on Schedule B (Part I, line 1) you report (for the first installment year) $807.50 in interest (8.5% x $9,500) instead of $475.00 (5% x $9,500). In other words, you pay tax on money that you will never receive: the 3.5% imputation. How does that grab you?

Investment Interest Limitation

Now, let's switch things around a bit. You are an avid investor with ideas and aspirations greater than your available cash. You borrow from friends, refinance your home, get a revolving line of credit from your bank, and set up a margin account with your broker. You use all of the borrowed money to acquire a much-expanded inventory of investments.

Naturally, you have to pay interest on this money. When you do pay said interest, it is characterized as *investment interest*. That is, it is interest paid in connection with property held for investment. Naturally, also, you want to take a tax deduction for the amount paid. For this, special tax treatment applies. Comes, now, Section 163(d): **Limitation on investment interest.**

In pertinent part, Section 163(d) reads as follows—

(1) In the case of a taxpayer other than a corporation, the amount allowed as a deduction . . . for investment interest for any taxable year shall not exceed the net investment income of the taxpayer for the taxable year.
(2) The amount not allowed as a deduction . . . by reason of paragraph (1) shall be treated as investment interest paid or accrued . . . in the succeeding taxable year.

The Section 163(d) rule goes on to point out that the disallowance feature does not apply to home mortgage "acquisition" indebtedness, equipment or inventory used in a trade or business, interest paid on rental real estate mortgages, and interest paid on personal loans such as for a car, furniture, boat, or vacation trip. Otherwise, if the borrowed money is used for profit-making investment purposes, the limitation rule applies.

Basically, the rule says that you cannot write off more in investment interest than your *net* investment income. Investment income consists of interest, dividends, annuities, royalties, certain distributions from partnerships, capital gain distributions (from mutual funds), capital gains on sales or exchanges, and ordinary gains from Section 1231 property. In lean years, your net investment income may not be enough to offset your total investment interest expense. In this case, your unused investment interest is carried over to subsequent years . . . until eventually used.

Where on your Form 1040 tax return do you claim your investment interest expense deduction?

More tax gimmickry awaits you.

First, you have to complete **Form 4952**: Investment Interest Expense Deduction. It's a short form with only six entry lines. The three most important lines are:

- *Total investment interest expense. (Current year plus prior-year carryforwards.)*
- *Net investment income . (See instructions.)*
- *Disallowed investment interest expense. (This amount is carried forward to ____.)*

The instructions tell you to enter your allowable deduction on Schedule A (Itemized Personal Deductions) where it is subject to still more limitations.

Our message here is quite simple. If you are a high-flyer-type investor, and you are leveraged to the hilt, don't expect to get any favorable tax treatment for your interest expense paid. You can, however, sidestep Section 163(d). As per Section 266: **Carrying charges**, you can elect to capitalize your total interest expense, providing you can allocate said expense, property by property.

Tax-Exempt Bonds

There is one particular type of investment that we have not commented on previously. It encompasses all of those debt instruments (bonds) issued by government agencies at all levels: federal, state, and local. Said instruments are issued, usually, in $10,000 increments and higher, with maturity dates ranging from a few months to 40 years. The interest rates paid range from about 3 to 4% for triple-A rated money market obligations to 7 to 8% for single-B and unrated long-term bonds.

As an investment class, State and local obligations are referred to as *municipal bonds*. They can be acquired as individual bonds or collectively as mutual fund shares. The individual bonds pay interest; the mutual fund shares pay interest dividends. A "State or local bond" means the obligation of a State or any political subdivision thereof. The term "State" includes the District of Columbia and any possession of the United States. The interest and dividend income from all public-purpose municipal bonds is Federal tax exempt.

The above is the gist of Section 103(a): **Interest on State and local bonds; Exclusion.** This section reads in part—

> *(a) Except as provided in subsection (b), **gross income does not include interest on any State or local bond**.*
> *(b) Subsection (a) shall not apply to* [any]—
> *(1) Private activity bond which is not a qualified bond . . .*
> *(2) Arbitrage bond . . .*
> *(3) Bond not in registered form . . .*
> [Emphasis added.]

It is important to be aware that any interest paid to you on Federal debt obligations (Savings bonds, Treasury notes, Ginnie

Maes, etc.) *is taxable* on Form 1040. Taxable also is any interest paid to you on foreign government debt obligations.

The classification of certain municipal bonds being tax-exempt means exactly that. The interest paid on said bonds is NOT REPORTED TO THE IRS! Yes, this is true. The paying agency does not have to file Form 1099-INT or 1099-DIV with our Big Brother.

But you know what? The IRS got around Section 163 and slipped one over on Congress. Commencing in 1984, the IRS required the reporting of all tax-exempt interest on page 1 of Form 1040. This inclusion is required even though the reported amount is not legally taxable. The IRS did this under the guise of including the tax-exempt income in the computational base for taxing your receipt of any Social Security benefits.

The line in question on page 1, Form 1040 now reads—

Tax-exempt interest income (see page _____).
DON'T include on line _____.

If you do not actually receive any Social Security benefits, then skip the tax-exempt line on Form 1040. There's already too much invasion of taxpayer financial privacy by the IRS.

If you sell or exchange municipal bonds or municipal fund shares, you compute and report the capital gain or loss just like any other stock or bond. The tax-exempt status applies only to the interest earned: **not** to the gain or loss at time of disposition. You cannot escape reporting muni-bond-disposition transactions on Schedule D.

Life Insurance & Annuities

Ordinarily, one doesn't think of life insurance, endowments, annuities, and annuity "wrap-arounds" as investments . . . but they are. They are contracts and contractual rights which increase in value at their maturity dates. Their increase in value is generated by the insurer who accepts your money, and reinvests that money into real estate, common stocks, corporate bonds, government bonds, mutual funds, money market instruments, certificates of deposit, and so on. Prior to their maturity dates, the contracts can be sold, exchanged, or surrendered. Any gain or loss at time of *sale or surrender* has to be tax reported. (If there are "like-kind" exchanges, no tax consequences arise.)

Life insurance is in a tax class of its own. It "matures" upon death of the insured. Proceeds paid by reason of death are income tax exempt: Section 101(a). (In some situations, the proceeds may be death taxed.) However, should the contract be sold or surrendered before its maturity, there is taxable gain to the extent that the cash surrender value exceeds the cumulative premiums or other consideration paid. Whether the gain is capital or ordinary depends on the relationship between the policy holder and the person insured. If there is a loss, the loss is not tax recognized. In the event of sale or surrender, the insurer reports the gross proceeds to the IRS via Form 1099-R: Total Distributions from . . . Insurance Contracts, Etc.

Endowments and annuities (fixed-contract type) are tax treated similarly. Both require that a fixed investment amount be paid on or before the contract starting date (maturity). The "starting date" is a specific living age of the beneficiary. The contracted payouts are taxed pursuant to an *exclusion ratio*, which is the upfront investment divided by the expected return under the contract. If the contract is sold, redeemed, or exchanged for life insurance **before** its starting date, there is capital gain or loss — relative to the invested amount — reportable on Schedule D.

Wrap-around annuities, also referred to as deferred variable annuities or tax-deferred annuities, are a special investment breed. When coupled with life insurance (the "wrap-around" aspect), they become a form of tax shelter. Premiums are variable, payouts are variable, and the purchaser usually has a choice between several closed-end mutual funds, and can exchange between them at will. As long as there are no contract sales, conversions, redemptions, or withdrawals before the contract payout date, the status quo remains. But if there are any withdrawals, distributions, loans, or pledging of the contract as security, before the purchaser attains age 59-1/2, a 10% *excise tax* applies. This excise tax is in addition to the regular tax on ordinary income. All said pre-age-59-1/2 distributions must be reported on **Form 5329**: Return for Additional Taxes Attributable to . . . Annuities and Modified Endowment Contracts.

Investing Globally

And, now, a few words about the latest "in thing" in investment circles: global investing. In theory, diversified investing in the approximately 175 sovereign nations of the world spreads your risks and increases your prospects for gain. In times of economic downturn in the U.S., not all sovereign nations will experience market declines simultaneously. Although there is some truth in the effects of "linkage" and "coupling," not all national economies function lock-step nor in tandem. Even in the worst of times, some nations will flourish . . . and some will not.

The total above-water land mass of the world is approximately 58 million square miles. In, on, and adjacent to this land, there is an abundance of natural resources for commercial development and distribution to approximately 5,000 million (5 billion) human beings. Thus, there is money to be made — and to be lost — in global visions.

Recognizing worldwide trends, most major U.S. banks, financial institutions, brokerage firms, mutual fund managements, and credit card establishments have "set up shop" in anticipation of the global interests of U.S. investors. Consequently, if you live, work, or retire in the United States, there is no need whatsoever for establishing separately, on your own, any foreign bank accounts, brokerage arrangements, trusts, or corporations. As an investor, your doing so raises certain tax suspicions. With IRS's mentality, the immediate suspicion is: What are you trying to hide? Are you involved in tax evasion, some covert business activity, or "tainted" drug money? Why didn't you complete Schedule B, Part III: Foreign Accounts and Foreign Trusts, on your Form 1040? (Recall the latter portions of Chapter 6: Portfolio Assets.)

Use Global Mutual Funds

As an individual investor, the ideal way to engage in international investments is through any of the 100 or so *global mutual funds*. These are U.S. corporations classed as "regulated investment companies" under the Internal Revenue Code: Sections 851 through 860. As such, these global funds pass through to each investor his/her prorata share of all income (interest, dividends, original issue and factoring discounts), capital gain distributions, and — most importantly — foreign taxes paid. Global funds are professionally managed and spread their risks by diversification among countries, commodities, real estate, manufacturers, businesses, and currencies. You can find out about global funds through financial journals and mutual fund guides.

Since this is a tax book, we think that the real advantage of global investing through mutual funds is that the nitty-gritty of record-keeping and accounting is done for you. Unless you instruct otherwise, the summary figures given to you are in U.S. dollars. This relieves you of keeping track of fluctuating foreign-currency exchange rates. Since each fund sends its annual Forms 1099 ("information returns") to the IRS, you are also relieved of that agency's innate suspicion of your foreign dealings.

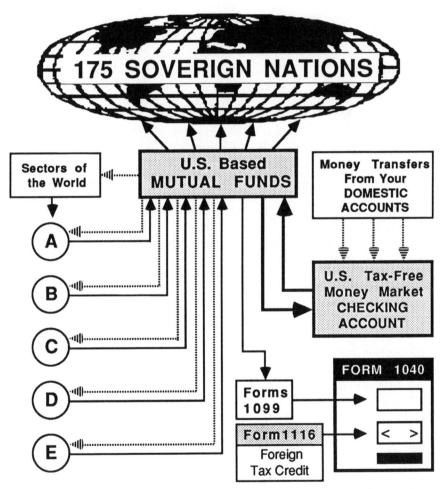

Fig. 12.3 - Investing Globally With Mutual Funds

Because mutual funds have "sector objectives," we suggest that you invest in no fewer than *three* global funds simultaneously. Even professional managers can misjudge the political and economic climate of a foreign country. Our vision in this regard is presented in Figure 12.3.

If you are going to invest globally in a big way, we also suggest that you set up a U.S. tax-free money market checking account for your foreign investing. Transfer the necessary funds from your domestic accounts in a way that is clearly traceable. Once your "seed money" is in the tax-free checking account (*in* the U.S.), make all of your foreign investments from this account. Conversely, when you redeem your foreign holdings, deposit said redemption money in the tax-free account. Since it will be earning interest/dividends tax-free in the U.S., there is no need to rush to re-invest it globally . . . until the right opportunity arises.

Meanwhile, you need to familiarize yourself with **Form 1116**: Computation of Foreign Tax Credit. To do so, request an official copy (and its instructions) from your nearest IRS office. When you look at Part II thereon: *Foreign Taxes Paid* — in foreign currency or U.S. dollars — you'll be glad of the Forms 1099 that the mutual fund management sent to you. Part III (of Form 1116) steps you through 13 entry lines for computing your foreign tax credit.

Your maximum computational credit is limited to the **ratio** of your taxable income (before exemptions) from sources within the U.S. In other words, you do not automatically get a direct offset against U.S. tax for each dollar of foreign tax paid. However, the amount of foreign tax uncredited in one year can be carried over to the next.

If you look at page 2 of your latest Form 1040, in the portion labeled: **Credits**, you'll see a line which reads—

Foreign tax credit (attach Form 1116)

Every dollar of foreign tax credit that you compute, reduces your U.S. tax, dollar-for-dollar. In this way, at least, foreign investing has its own special rewards.

ABOUT
THE AUTHOR

Holmes F. Crouch

Born on a small farm in southern Maryland, Holmes was graduated from the U.S. Coast Guard Academy with a Bachelor's Degree in Marine Engineering. While serving on active duty, he wrote many technical articles on maritime matters. After attaining the rank of Lieutenant Commander, he resigned to pursue a career as a nuclear engineer.

Continuing his education, he earned a Master's Degree in Nuclear Engineering from the University of California. He also authored two books on nuclear propulsion. As a result of the tax write-offs associated with writing these books, the IRS audited his returns. The IRS's handling of the audit procedure so annoyed Holmes that he undertook to become as knowledgeable as possible regarding tax procedures. He became a licensed private Tax Practitioner by passing an examination administered by the IRS. Having attained this credential, he started his own tax preparation and counseling business in 1972.

In the early years of his tax practice, he was a regular talk-show guest on San Francisco's KGO Radio responding to hundreds of phone-in tax questions from listeners. He was a much sought-after guest speaker at many business seminars and taxpayer meetings. He also provided counseling on special tax problems, such as divorce matters, property exchanges, timber harvesting, mining ventures, animal breeding, independent contractors, selling businesses, and offices-at-home. Over the past 20 years, he has prepared nearly 9,000 tax returns for individuals, estates, and small businesses.

During the tax season of January through April, he prepares returns in a unique manner. During a single meeting, he completes the return . . . *on the spot!* The client leaves with his return signed, sealed, and in a stamped envelope. His unique approach to preparing returns and his personal interest in his clients' tax affairs have honed his professional proficiency. His expertise extends through itemized deductions, computer-matching of income sources, capital gains and losses, business expenses and cost of goods, residential rental expenses, limited and general partnership activities, closely-held corporations, to family farms and ranches.

He remembers spending 12 straight hours completing a doctor's complex return. The next year, the doctor, having moved away, utilized a large accounting firm to prepare his return. Their accountant was so impressed by the manner in which the prior return was prepared that he recommended the doctor travel the 500 miles each year to have Holmes continue doing it.

He recalls preparing a return for an unemployed welder, for which he charged no fee. Two years later the welder came back and had his return prepared. He paid the regular fee . . . and then added a $300 tip.

During the off season, he represents clients at IRS audits and appeals. In one case a shoe salesman's audit was scheduled to last three hours. However, after examining Holmes' documentation it was concluded in 15 minutes with "no change" to his return. In another instance he went to an audit of a custom jeweler that the IRS dragged out for more than six hours. But, supported by Holmes' documentation, the client's return was accepted by the IRS with "no change."

Then there was the audit of a language translator that lasted two full days. The auditor scrutinized more than $1.25 million in gross receipts, all direct costs, and operating expenses. Even though all expensed items were documented and verified, the auditor decided that more than $23,000 of expenses ought to be listed as capital items for depreciation instead. If this had been enforced it would have resulted in a significant additional amount of tax. Holmes strongly disagreed and after many hours explanation got the amount reduced by more than 60% on behalf of his client.

He has dealt extensively with gift, death and trust tax returns. These preparations have involved him in the tax aspects of wills, estate planning, trustee duties, probate, marital and charitable bequests, gift and death exemptions, and property titling.

Although not an attorney, he prepares Petitions to the U.S. Tax Court for clients. He details the IRS errors and taxpayer facts by citing pertinent sections of tax law and regulations. In a recent case involving an attorney's ex-spouse, the IRS asserted a tax deficiency of $155,000. On behalf of his client, he petitioned the Tax Court and within six months the IRS conceded the case.

Over the years, Holmes has observed that the IRS is not the industrious, impartial, and competent federal agency that its official public imaging would have us believe.

He found that, at times, under the slightest pretext, the IRS has interpreted against a taxpayer in order to assess maximum penalties, and may even delay pending matters so as to increase interest due on additional taxes. He has confronted the IRS in his own behalf on five separate occasions, going before the U.S. Claims Court, U.S. District Court, and U.S. Tax Court. These were court actions that tested specific sections of the Internal Revenue Code which he found ambiguous, inequitable, and abusively interpreted by the IRS.

Disturbed by the conduct of the IRS and by the general lack of tax knowledge by most individuals, he began an innovative series of taxpayer-oriented Federal tax guides. To fulfill this need, he undertook the writing of a series of guidebooks that provide in-depth knowledge on one tax subject at a time. He focuses on subjects that plague taxpayers all throughout the year. Hence, his formulation of the "Allyear" Tax Guides. This book is one in the series. Several have already been completed (see listing on next page) and others are in process.

The author is indebted to his wife, Irma Jean, and daughter, Barbara MacRae, for the word processing and computer graphics that turn his experiences into the reality of these publications. Holmes welcomes comments, questions, and suggestions from his readers. He can be contacted through the publisher.

ALLYEAR
TAX GUIDES IN PRINT

Series 100 - INDIVIDUALS AND FAMILIES

    101 - Tax Guide: BEING SELF-EMPLOYED
    102 - Tax Guide: BUSINESS AUTO & TRAVEL
    104 - Tax Guide: RESOLVING DIVORCE ISSUES

Series 200 - INVESTORS AND BUSINESSES

    201 - Tax Guide: INVESTOR GAINS & LOSSES
    203 - Tax Guide: STARTING YOUR BUSINESS

Series 300 - RETIREES AND ESTATES

    303 - Tax Guide: WRITING YOUR WILL
    304 - Tax Guide: YOUR EXECUTOR DUTIES

Series 400 - OWNERS AND SELLERS

    401 - Tax Guide: RENTAL REAL ESTATE
    403 - Tax Guide: SELLING YOUR HOME

Series 500 - AUDITS AND APPEALS

    502 - Tax Guide: WINNING YOUR AUDIT
    503 - Tax Guide: DISAGREEING WITH THE IRS
    504 - Tax Guide: GOING INTO TAX COURT

To obtain any of the above 12 books,
contact your local bookstore or bookseller.

Otherwise, phone or write to:

Allyear Tax Guides
20484 Glen Brae Dr.
Saratoga, CA   95070

Phone: (408) 867-2628